THE CANARY ISLANDS

John and Anne Mason

THE CANARY ISLANDS

B. T. Batsford Ltd
London

First Published 1976
© John and Anne Mason 1976
Computer typeset by Input Typesetting Ltd., 4 Valentine
Place, London S.E.1
Made and printed in Great Britain by
Biddles Ltd, Guildford, Surrey
for the publishers B. T. Batsford Ltd, 4 Fitzhardinge Street,
London W1H 0AH

ISBN 0 7134 3104 0

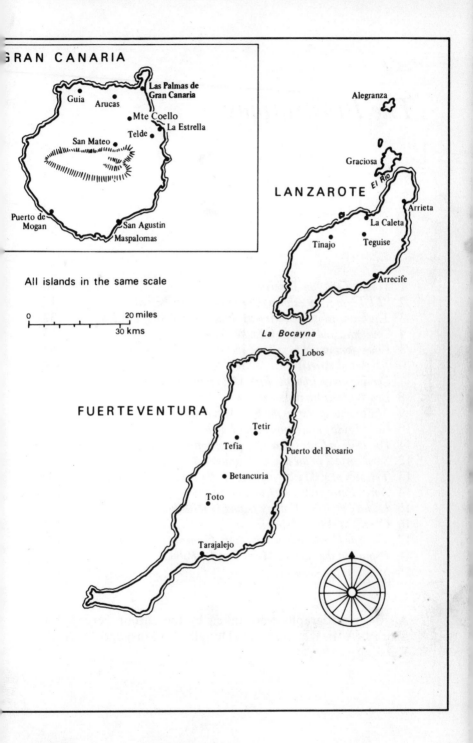

GRAN CANARIA

Las Palmas de Gran Canaria

Guia
Arucas
Mte Coello
La Estrella
San Mateo
Telde

Puerto de Mogan
San Agustin
Maspalomas

All islands in the same scale

0   20 miles
          30 kms

Alegranza

Graciosa

LANZAROTE
El Rio

Arrieta
La Caleta
Tinajo   Teguise

Arrecife

La Bocayna

Lobos

FUERTEVENTURA
Tetir
Tefia
Puerto del Rosario
Betancuria
Toto

Tarajalejo

The Illustrations

All the photographs were taken by the authors, except for figure 1 (A. F. Kersting), 11 (Douglas Dickins) and 14 (A. F. Kersting).

1. Introduction

When arriving at a strange island where one intends to stay for a time the most exciting approach is always by sea. The vision of somewhere new gradually rises from the horizon, then as one sails nearer, the land-mass slowly takes shape into mountains and valleys, buildings and gardens, all waiting to be explored in the future.

So it was when we first arrived at Las Palmas, capital and main port of Grand Canary, one of the Fortunate Isles of the ancients, but today known as the Canary Islands.

Situated in the Atlantic Ocean, the nearest island being some 60 miles off the north-west coast of Africa; between 27 and 29 degrees north latitude, and 13 and 18 degrees west longitude, they are provinces of Spain, which the Canarios refer to as the Peninsula.

Here the official language is Spanish, the currency is Spanish, the manners and customs are Spanish – even the climate is similar to Spain although the islands are some 700 miles south-west of the mother country.

The whole archipelago consists of seven main islands, Grand Canary, Tenerife, La Palma, Fuerteventura, El Hierro, La Gomero, and Lanzarote with its three small satellites, Lobos, Alegranza and Graciosa – this last the only one of the three which is inhabited.

We wanted to see them all, find out as much about them as we could, for there was very little written about them in those days, which was strange for islands on the main shipping routes between Africa and South America. And except for

Grand Canary and Tenerife, very few people visited them. We wanted to increase those visitors by two.

Arriving in Las Palmas today is very different to when we sailed into Puerto de la Luz for the first time in 1960. The bare rugged hills in the background are still there, but today's high-rise buildings along the extending line of the city had then hardly started to grow.

It would have been late autumn in England. If we had been home in London we would have been bundled up in warm clothing and probably moaning about the cold weather ahead. But here in the Canary Islands, land of Primavera Eterna – Eternal Spring, we strolled in the sunshine in summer cottons, revelled in the sight of tropical gardens ablaze with colour, and swam in the Atlantic, which here is warmed by the Gulf Stream.

We travelled around the city and nearer villages in the rickety old buses, called in the islands gua-guas (you pronounce it waa-waas), a name which is supposed to have been brought back from Venezuela by those Canarios who migrated there, and then returned to their home land.

In those days the city bus fare was equivalent to one-half of a new penny.

Everywhere we were welcomed, especially when we said we were planning an indefinite stay and not just a week or two between ships, for the Canarios are very proud of their islands and appreciate people who want to spend time in getting to know them.

British people have for long been welcomed to these islands, and when A. Samler Brown wrote his first guide to the Canary Islands (which he combined in his book with Madeira and the Azores) at the end of the nineteenth century, he wrote it as a 'Practical and Complete Guide for the use of tourists and invalids'.

For many English people of means were sent here by their doctors to convalesce after illness – the combination of sea voyage and the climate of the islands usually proving most successful in effecting a cure, as well as being most enjoyable for them.

Retired people soon realised the advantages of both Tenerife and Grand Canary as pleasant inexpensive places to spend the winter months, and as there were a number of British shipping lines calling at the islands, there was no difficulty with transport.

But it was not until the great 1960s boom in packaged holidays that first Las Palmas and then Puerto de la Cruz became really known to tourists from Britain and Europe.

Trade connections with England go back to the sixteenth century, when there were English factors or agents representing London Merchants in Grand Canary for the purchase of sugar and wine – the Canary sack was very popular.

In 1883-4 submarine cables brought the archipelago into close connection with the rest of the world.

Ships from Britain and the Continent going to West and South Africa, and South America and the West Indies, found the islands useful ports of call. Modern coaling stations were set up in both Las Palmas and Santa Cruz de Tenerife, and the harbours were extended to provide greater facilities for handling cargo.

At first it was largely one-way trade, with coal and some merchandise in small quantities being brought to the islands, and a number of British firms established offices at both ports to handle this trade.

One of these was Sir Alfred Jones, a shrewd Liverpool shipping man, who came to Las Palmas to establish a coaling station for his firm, Elder Dempster & Co. He soon realised there were also other opportunities for his company, and arranged for his ships to return to England carrying cargoes of bananas, which were then, as now, the largest crop produced in the islands, as well as tomatoes and potatoes.

In 1888 he took as his partner a young Englishman named Pavillard, who was already living in Las Palmas. Later they went into partnership with another British firm of fruit exporters, Fyffes, the company being known as Elders & Fyffes Ltd. Other English companies were soon established, such as Yeowards, Hamiltons and Blandys (better known in

Madeira), and British shipping companies such as Union Castle and Royal Mail Lines were represented.

Those names are still prominent today in the islands' business communities, and we well know the mahogany-panelled office at the entrance to the Santa Catalina quay which houses Elder Dempster (Canary Islands) Ltd, looking very much as it did in Sir Alfred Jones' day with its old leather-bound shipping registers and splendid models of old steam ships.

Today, Eugene Pavillard in Las Palmas and Louis Pavillard in Santa Cruz still run the family business, which now has many ramifications in both islands. With their younger brother, Dr Stanley Pavillard and his attractive Australian wife, they have all been good friends of ours over the years, always ready with both information and hospitality whenever we have been in the Canaries.

Between the two world wars there were some 500 English residents in Las Palmas; there are probably more than that today. When we lived in Santa Cruz, the then British consul, the late Mr Eric Fox, always had a party at his home on the Queen's birthday, and we were always surprised to see how many British people turned up to drink 'A health unto Her Majesty'. Most of them had lived there quietly for many years, and this was one day they all got together.

Much as we enjoyed the sunshine and general air of 'Mañana', we had not come to the islands just to laze around Las Palmas. We wanted to get to know all the islands, and in the next six months we visited them all, sometimes travelling in the most uncomfortable conditions. Like the time we went from las Palmas to Santa Cruz de Tenerife in an unpleasant 800-ton ship called the Lanzarote, which pitched and tossed through a howling gale all the way. Every time the officers wanted a meal we were evicted from the only saloon out on a rain-swept deck – fortunately we are good sailors.

But we saw some fantastic scenery, met many pleasant hospitable people, and had a few adventures along the way. They were happy, carefree days, and without too much effort we were always able to get enough work done to keep our editors happy, for writing has always been our main source of income.

But after six months we had to return to England, and when we sailed away it was one of our saddest departures – and we have had many over the years. We did not anticipate a return here in the near future, for our paper in Australia was expecting us home within the year.

But when we were at last due to go back to Australia we found the attractions of Britain and Europe too strong to resist. How could we give up those long weekends in Paris and Brussels, just across the Channel; our trips to the Swiss Alps; wouldn't we miss the streets of London; the theatres and the whole cosmopolitan atmosphere? And our English publishers wanted a couple of books – we couldn't possibly go 12,000 miles away from all this.

Instead, we returned to the Canaries, for we couldn't forget the sunshine of the islands, just the right place for writing a book or two. And it was near enough for our son to come down for his holidays from boarding school, for he always joined us at holiday times wherever our travels took us.

This time we decided to settle down in one spot, so we rented a delightful little house with all 'mod cons' in a Canario setting just two miles from Puerto de la Cruz – everybody calls it Puerto – and prepared to make it our home for the winter.

We planned our work to fit in with the life of the islanders, both Canarios and those expatriates from many different countries who had settled here, and were our friends.

Writing each morning, lunch, a siesta, another hour's work, then down to the plaza for a drink under the trees and a chat with acquaintances at nearby tables.

Or there might be pre-dinner drinks at the home of a friend, a barbecue party, or people coming to us for a buffet meal. It was a pleasant life, and in those days living was cheap there.

We still travelled round the islands, going back to places we had known from our previous visit and discovering new ones. But things were changing, at least in the two major islands of Grand Canary and Tenerife. The tourists were increasing in numbers as packaged tours became more popular.

Grandiose developments were being planned, high-rise hotels being built, there was talk of new resorts being built around the coast, and more and more people were coming here to cash in on the tourist boom.

We wondered how it would affect the people of the islands, the simple country people with their easy-going ways and philosophic attitudes to life. They were poor, for the most part, but this didn't seem to worry them unduly; they worked cheerfully and we always found them friendly, ready to help strangers, and always pleased to be greeted with a few words in Spanish, no matter how limited your conversation.

Then at the end of 1962, it came to an end. Once again the time came when we had to go back to England. We packed up all the bits and pieces we had accumulated after more than a year in our little house; did a round of our friends to say 'goodbye', and made a last tour of Puerto, which had been hardly more than a village when we had first seen it two and a half years before, but was now a popular tourist resort.

We knew a rapid change was taking place and these islands would never be the same again, and we were glad we had seen them before they became too changed, too tourist-conscious.

So our dream of perhaps settling there came to an end. But not our connection with the islands, for we have been back a number of times since then – our last visit was only a few months ago.

Every time we return we see more changes, changes we view with mixed feelings, for it is stupid to be too nostalgic about the past. The tourist industry has sprouted here as probably nowhere else except around the Spanish mainland coasts. Places that were lonely deserts not much more than ten years ago are now modern luxury playgrounds, some pleasing and tasteful, others garish and tawdry, at least in our eyes, remembering our early impressions of these islands.

But behind this tourist facade the hinterland has changed but little, and life for the country people goes on much as it has always done. Or perhaps we should say as it has always been for the older generation, for the young ones have found new opportunities for employment in the hotels and shops catering to the tourists. And with the visitors has come one important difference – the prosperity brought by tourism has overspread into village life, people are generally better off, life is more comfortable and their children have more opportunities for the future.

And the sun-starved people of Britain and northern Europe have new sunshine playgrounds available to them at reasonable prices in these Fortunate Isles.

In the following pages we have tried to give a picture of those islands as they are today – a picture perhaps tinged with something of our nostalgia from our very pleasant association with them, which we hope will continue for many more visits.

2. History

The existence of the Canary Islands has been known to Europeans for perhaps some 3,000 years, but their history, in a practical sense, really did not start until less then six centuries ago, in the beginning of the fifteenth century.

They appear under many names in the myths and legends of the ancient Phoenicians, Carthaginians, Greeks and Romans.

Homeric legends referred to them as the Elysian Fields beyond the Pillars of Hercules to which were sent the souls of dead heroes. They existed on the edge of the world and were a place to which winter never came; even to the ancients apparently, they were a land of Primavera Eterna, Eternal Spring.

Herodotus described the islands as the Gardens of the Hesperides where grew the golden apples; some legends say they were guarded by dragons breathing out fire (volcanoes, perhaps). Here Atlas on his cone-shaped mountain supported the heavens on his shoulders – which could be a reference to the mountain of Teide on Tenerife.

Many have suggested that they might be the remains of Atlantis, to which Plato referred when writing of that lost continent, which was suddenly submerged in one day and one night, and on sinking all life disappeared, leaving a sea of mire in which shoals emerged, presenting grave dangers to seafarers.

Coming down to Roman times we are on rather firmer ground, where facts, if somewhat nebulous, sometimes emerge from fiction. They called them the Insulae Fortunatae, the

1 *(opposite) Mount Teide, on Tenerife.*

Fortunate Isles, by which name they are often referred to today.

What exactly the Romans knew about the islands is not exactly clear, but King Juba II of Mauretania (he reigned from about 25 B.C. to 25 A.D.), a satellite kingdom of the Roman Empire, made a report to the Emperor Augustus telling of an expedition he had sent to investigate the islands, but the news they brought back was not very detailed.

The expedition visited one or two islands, probably Fuerteventura and Lanzarote, the two nearest to the African coast, where they found no human inhabitants but discovered a number of large and ferocious dogs, two of which they brought back with them and presented to the king.

He named the islands after the dogs, Canaria, a derivation of the Latin word for dog, Canis; the first time this name was applied to the islands.

Then they disappeared from recorded history until about the year 1,000, when the Arab geographer, Edrisi, describes a voyage by adventurers from Lisbon who visited the islands; however, what is fact and what is invention in this account is open to question.

In 1291 two ships were sent from Genoa by the powerful Doria family to find and explore the islands. If the crews did land there was never known, for the ships never returned, but it is thought they might have reached the islands before being lost later.

Early in the fourteenth century it was definitely established that the islands were inhabited by a race of light-coloured aborigines, called Guanches. During that century many visits were paid by Spanish and Portuguese ships, but these were to capture slaves, this being a thriving trade of the period.

This also led to disputes between the two countries concerning suzerainty of the archipelago, and in 1344 a Castilian nobleman, Count Louis de la Cerda, was crowned King of the Fortunate Isles by the Avignonese Pope Clement VI. But this was an empty title and it is doubtful if the Count ever visited his 'kingdom'.

Then in 1402 a Norman nobleman, Jean de Bethencourt,

2 *(opposite)* "*El Tigre*", *the cannon which shot off Nelson's arm.*

and a Poitevan, Gadifer de la Salle, fitted out an expedition to conquer the islands, convert the natives to Christianity and establish their own empire, although this would be under the overlordship of the King of Castile, the King of France having refused to assist them.

They landed in Lanzarote in July 1402, and built a fort they called Rubicon, and set about the task of overrunning Lanzarote and the rest of the archipelago.

History had come to the Fortunate Isles, or the Islas Canarias, the long-forgotten name coined by Juba II.

The natives, the Guanches, on both Lanzarote and Fuerteventura were at first inclined to be friendly and hospitable to the invaders, and although acts of cruelty and the taking of many of the natives as slaves led to some resistance, Bethencourt had both islands completely under his control within three years.

Eventually Bethencourt and Gadifer quarreled, with the former having his claims upheld by the court of Castile (the kingdom of Castile formed the nucleus of what later would be the kingdom of Spain) and Gadifer leaving. In 1405 Bethencourt returned to his native Normandy to raise funds for further ships and men to extend his conquests, but failed in this, and died an impoverished and embittered man in 1425.

For the next half-century the history of the islands is confused, but during that period Gomera and Hierro were also conquered and occupied by members of the Herrara family, who were made Counts of Gomera. Their domain included the four islands already conquered, and they acknowledged the suzerainty of the King of Castile, to whom they also paid tribute.

An attempt was made to take over La Palma, but this proved abortive; no attempt was made at that time on either of the major islands, Grand Canary and Tenerife, whose inhabitants were reported to be numerous, warlike and very ferocious, a daunting prospect to the Lords of Gomera with their limited resources.

But in 1464 they decided to send a force from Gomera to set up a trading post at Anaga on Tenerife, and establish a military base there. Relations with the natives were at first friendly, but later became strained and they were forced to abandon the project.

Grand Canary had suffered some sporadic attacks from Herrara forces, none of them successful; but in April 1478 Juan Rejón, an experienced soldier sent to subdue the islands by Ferdinand of Castile, landed with his forces at Las Palmas.

He won a victory over the Guanches at the battle of Guiniguada, but matters were complicated by dissensions on both sides, the Spanish leaders quarreling among themselves, as did the native chieftains. Rejón was later killed in a skirmish in Gomera and he was replaced by a veteran of the Moorish wars, Pedro de Vera, who was later joined by another veteran soldier, Alonso Fernandez de Lugo.

The campaign dragged on for several years with successes on both sides, until a detachment of Vera's forces was defeated with considerable losses at the Battle of Ajodar. Vera regrouped his forces, and learning from his defeat, refused to be drawn again into open conflict, but instead attacked the Guanches, driving them from one stronghold to another until they were convinced they could not hope to win, and they finally surrendered on 29 April 1483.

Further attempts at conquering the other islands were delayed for nearly ten years until September 1491, when de Lugo invaded La Palma with a force supported by natives recruited in Gomera and some tribes from La Palma who had already defected to him. This campaign lasted eight months, prolonged to this length by one tribe which strategically established itself in the crater of Taburiente, an almost impregnable position. They were finally defeated by being lured out on promises of peace, then were treacherously attacked.

In April 1493, de Lugo landed at Anaga (Santa Cruz) in Tenerife, in order to subdue the last remaining island. After some initial success his force was crushingly defeated at the Battle of La Matanza, where he suffered terrible losses, and he was forced to evacuate the island in June 1494.

He returned in November the same year and this time

inflicted an equally crushing defeat on the Guanches at the Battle of La Victoria, in which large numbers of their men were slain.

That was the beginning of the end for the aborigine defenders, and although there was sporadic fighting for the next two years, there was no organised resistance. Sick of the fighting and weakened by a mysterious disease called the *madorra* – which not only took away their will to fight but also their will to live – the Guanches offered little opposition, and eventually capitulated on 29 September 1496.

At last, 94 years after de Bethencourt had landed on Lanzarote, the conquest of all the islands was completed. De Lugo was hailed as the hero of the day, called the Conquistador of the Canaries and given the hereditary title of Adelantado (Governor) of the whole archipelago.

The office of Adelantado remained supreme until 1536, when powers were vested directly in the crown. The Harrara family (sometimes known as Peraza, as Herrara's son adopted his mother's name of Peraza) continued to administer their four islands as a feudal estate, but owing allegiance to the Spanish crown, until late in the eighteenth century when they became part of metropolitan Spain.

This despite the fact that the widow of a Lord of Gomera, Ferdinand Peraza the Younger, married de Lugo and went to live in Tenerife for a time. That widow was the famous, or rather infamous, Beatriz de Bobadilla who was reputed to have had an affair with Columbus – but more of that later.

The history of the Canaries following the conquest, although generally peaceful, has had its moments of excitement. In their first two hundred years or so under Spanish rule the islands suffered numerous raids from Moorish pirates who were always eventually beaten off, but on occasions, only after they had caused considerable damage and sometimes killed many of the defenders, and carried off others into slavery.

Lanzarote and Gomera were the worst sufferers, and it is reported that Jarife, King of Fez, occupied Lanzarote in 1569 and again in 1586, claiming possession by virtue of his descent from the King of Mauritania. He was, however, forced to retire, carrying with him a number of prisoners.

There were also attacks by European pirates and privateers, as well as by various naval squadrons, including some British.

Sir Francis Drake and Sir John Hawkins made an unsuccessful attack on Las Palmas in 1595, and in 1656 Admiral Sir Robert Blake attacked Santa Cruz de Tenerife with 36 ships, causing serious damage. Another English attack was made in 1743 by Admiral Sir Charles Winton, and finally the most famous, that by Nelson in 1797, when he suffered the only defeat of his career and lost his arm. (See under Tenerife, page 00.)

In 1821 the Canary Islands were created a province of Spain, with Santa Cruz de Tenerife as the capital and seat of government, a decision which caused much jealousy in Las Palmas.

Until 1927 the archipelago was administered as one province, but then they were divided in two; Grand Canary, comprising Grand Canary, Fuerteventura and Lanzarote, with Las Palmas as the capital; and Tenerife Province with Tenerife, La Palma, Gomera and Hierro, with Santa Cruz de Tenerife as capital.

Each had a Governor and Captain General, Francisco Franco holding that latter office in Tenerife immediately prior to the Spanish Civil War, which it may be said, really started here in the Canaries.

For, although the islands were not actively engaged in the Civil War of 1936–9, except for those men who went to the Peninsula to fight, it was here that Franco and his officers planned the start of the revolution against the Republican government of Spain.

The Guanches. While the history of the Canary Islands until comparatively recent times was obscure, so is the origin of those aboriginal inhabitants, the Guanches, whom the fourteenth- and fifteenth-century invaders found living on the islands. Where they came from and at what period is still a matter of some controversy, although authorities agree on many points.

When the Europeans arrived they found a race of people described as being rather tall, well built and of great physical strength. Many were fair-skinned (the word 'white' has been used), with blond hair and sometimes with blue eyes.

Some records say there were houses here, but for the most part they appear to have been cave-dwellers. Theirs was a Neolithic culture, their tools being of stone and they used utensils of crude pottery, generally plain and undecorated. Their agriculture was primitive and the only animals on the islands seemed to be goats and dogs. They wore clothes of either skins or grasses sewn together with fibres.

They had no written language, so that such legends and folklore that they may have had were handed down from generation to generation by word of mouth. And as those early Spanish visitors were only interested in conquest and slaves and not in the culture of such a backward and untutored people they failed to keep any adequate records of the Guanche culture.

These aboriginal people had a class system with kings and chiefs, princely families and nobles – and the ordinary people. They worshipped a single Supreme Deity to whom they made offerings of goats' milk. Also, on several of the islands they mummified their dead; examples of these can be seen in the Archaeological Museums of both Las Palmas and Santa Cruz de Tenerife.

Described as a gentle and hospitable people, they were, nevertheless, trained in the arts of war; doubtless with their social structure they had internicine struggles – but not inter-island conflicts.

Although they had similar languages and cultures and were apparently of the same stock, the inhabitants of each island were ignorant of the people of the others – probably even of their existence. For although at some time they must have come from across the seas, these people had lost the art of navigation; in fact, they had no boats, did not know how to make them, and knew nothing of the sea or navigation, an incredible thing for people on such small islands.

Nowhere else in the world will you find a group of islands where the original inhabitants did not make even a crude dugout canoe or a coracle made of skins such as was made by the ancient Britons – and both these would surely have been within the scope of the Guanche capabilities.

Then from where did they come and when?

The most logical answer is from North Africa, the nearest mainland. The most accepted theory is that they were of Berber stock. Scientific evidence shows that the skulls which have been found are of the Cro-Magnon type, similar to those of Berbers. Their language also bore a strong resemblance to that spoken by Berber tribes.

The fact that they mummified their dead, a practice known to the Egyptians 4,000 years ago, suggests they may have originated from a people who would have practised this rite, as the early Berbers may have done.

When? Various investigations have resulted in a variety of approximate dates. Their culture and standard of civilisation suggests the early Christina era, probably some time during the first or second centuries.

But whatever their origins the Guanches as a separate people are no more – for their language, customs and identity disappeared in the years that followed the conquest of the islands. Many had been slain in the fighting, thousands were shipped to Spain to be sold into slavery, and many of those who did remain in the islands became slaves to their conquerors. Those who remained free were absorbed into the Spanish community, and there were numbers of cases of noble Guanche maidens marrying Spaniards.

Modern anthropologists agree that the Guanche strain can still be seen today throughout the islands, particularly among the country people. Skull formations and general characteristics prove this. But today they are all Canarios, Spanish Canarios, whose habits, customs and language, and usually their names, are Spanish.

But there are still some with Guanche names, just as there are many Guanche names for towns and villages all over the archipelago.

And there are remains of their culture to be seen. Hundreds of the caves they occupied are still to be found. Some are in use as warehouses or stables for stock; some have been converted into dwellings for modern Canarios (and good homes they make, too, as we shall see later); and a few of the more important have been protected as ancient monuments.

Some of their burial grounds have also been preserved, such as the one near Galdar, in Grand Canary.

One custom the Guanches bequeathed to the conquerors was the whistling language used in Gomera, and which still has a limited use in the rugged interior. This was improved and adapted by the settlers to make use of Spanish words and phrases as a unique form of communication, as described in the chapter on Gomera.

3. Food and Wine

Good restaurants and hotels in the Canaries pride themselves on their high standard of international cuisine, although there is, not surprisingly, a tendency for Spanish dishes to play an important part in most menus.

Local fish, fruit and vegetables are excellent, but as much of the meat has to be imported it is expensive, and not always first-grade. Locally raised pork is the best of the meat obtainable, and *cochinillo asado* (roast sucking pig) and *cabrito asado* (roast kid) are served for special occasions. Rabbits also play an important part in Canario menus.

The good fishing grounds around the islands, those between the African coast and Lanzarote and Fuerteventura being the richest, produce a variety of tasty fish, most of it with names strange to British ears. *Mero* and *cherna* are a type of rock bass and are excellent eating; *merluza* is the Spanish name for hake; swordfish and tunny (*atun*) steaks are well worth trying when they are obtainable; dried cod (*bacalao*) is popular for a number of dishes, especially when served with *mojo*. *Calamares* and *pulpo* are an experience if you can forget you are eating squid or baby octopus — we like the crisply fried *calamares* usually served as *tapas* in many of the bars.

Those who are familiar with Spain will know of the tasty *tapas* or small serves of savoury foods served with drinks in bars, and this is a custom also followed in the Canaries.

The basis of country meals all over the archipelago is *gofio*, a flour made from ground corn which has first been roasted. Most farmers dry their home-grown corn on the flat roofs of their houses, the golden ears hanging like tassels in the sun, usually with strings of red peppers drying alongside, making a colourful contrast. The corn is then taken to a local mill to be roasted and ground.

When travelling through country districts you may notice the distinctive smell of the roasting corn from the *gofio* mills. In the old days this was done at home, the corn then being ground between two rounds of stone turned by a handle, and there are still some of these ancient handmills to be seen in old houses or museums (see page 00).

It is believed that *gofio* was the staple food of the Guanches, but they used wheat, for corn was unknown before the discovery of America. Today other grains are also used as available.

Gofio is used in a variety of ways, and in many dishes is served with a particularly fiery sauce known as *mojo picon*, made with chili peppers, garlic, oil, vinegar, salt and pepper, ground to a thin paste with a mortar and pestle.

There is a saying that you can tell the quality – and hotness – of *mojo* immediately you taste it. If it is good it first makes your eyes water, then it makes you swear! Another milder type of *mojo* is made with parsley, coriander and green peppers instead of chilis, and this *mojo verdi* is very good, especially with fish.

To taste *gofio* today it is necessary to go into the country districts and eat either with a family or at one of the small inns. Fish is coated with it before frying, and soups are thickened with it, especially *potaje*, the fresh vegetable soups which make such good filling meals. It is mixed with the local white goats' milk cheese – *queso blanca* – into small balls and served with *mojo*, or made into a thick, sweet porridge, sprinkled with cinnamon, as a pudding.

In Fuerteventura the most popular cheese is made with half goats' milk and half ewes' milk. It is packed into round baskets of plaited palm leaves and dried in the sun and wind for two or three days.

Excellent potatoes are grown in the islands (rather surprisingly, we were told that Irish seed potatoes produced the best crops in the islands), and a popular way of cooking them is in their skins in heavily salted water, or preferably in sea water, when they are known as *papas arrugadas*, or wrinkled potatoes.

These can make a meal when served with *mojo* or *queso blanca,* and farm workers who cannot get home for the mid-day meal often take a basket of these instead. We first tasted these potatoes and their accompanying *mojo* years ago when we were picnicking at San Marco beach, near Icod. The Canario family sitting next to us insisted that we, as visitors, should share their meal, and produced a great basket of *papas arrugadas*, kept hot in a spotlessly clean cotton cloth, and accompanied by a jar of a particularly fiery *mojo*. Fortunately we had been previously warned about the *mojo* and took only a very tentative taste, but we enjoyed the potatoes and the deliciously fresh tomatoes and the white cheese which came with them.

I am sure our new friends also enjoyed the novelty of our canned-ham sandwiches and hard-boiled eggs which we shared with them in return.

Fish is plentiful and used in many ways by the Canarios, and also in the hotels – although here the chefs are inclined to be more conservative. *Caldo de Pescado* is a tasty fish soup, while *Sancocho de Pescado* is a fish stew, usually made with dried, boiled cod and potatoes, flavoured with *mojo* and thickened with *gofio*. Fish steaks are cooked in a casserole with potatoes, onions, tomatoes, peppers and garlic under the name of *Cazuela Canario*.

When we lived in Puerto we would regularly visit the fish market, which in those days was simply two rows of stone counters beside the old port. The fishing boats would unload their catch direct into the waiting hands of a dozen or so stalwart fish-wives, who then cleaned and sold the fish on the spot.

As an enthusiastic cook, Anne liked to discuss ways of cooking the various fish on sale, and her favourite fish-wife, Carmencita, was always ready to suggest the local dishes and how they were prepared. We liked fish soup, and she would always keep the best pieces for us as well as the fish heads, which were an important part of the recipe, but which none of the other foreign community ever used.

One day Carmencita startled the other customers, and especially the foreigners, by loudly calling out, 'Ah-ha, Señora, I have the Baroness's head for you today.'

The Baroness was a neighbour of ours who had then been living in Puerto for more than twenty years, and was a very well-known personality in the town. It took some explaining to convince a few people that between us and Carmencita there were no murderous plans concerning our neighbour.

Today there is a modern fish-market at the end of the port which is not nearly so friendly, but then it is much more progressive with freezers and modern methods of cleanliness. Personally, we would rather have the old friendly fish-wives.

Some of the best of real Canario dishes are served in the Paradors, the government-owned hotels, on the various islands, and we have always found the cooks here most helpful in explaining the dishes and their ingredients when they see you are interested. One traditional dish which is only served on special occasions is *Puchero Canario de las Siete Carnes,* or Canary stew of the seven meats. This contains a somewhat unusual mixture of beef, pork, veal, rabbit, chicken, pigeon and partridge, but as we were never at the right place on such special occasions we never did taste it.

A delicious soup is *Potaje de Berros,* made with fresh watercress and herbs. A typical dish we enjoyed at the Parador de Tejeda was *Conejo Embarrado,* rabbit baked in a savoury sauce and served in individual pottery dishes piping hot from the oven. Here also we had a delicious sweet, *Bienmesabe de Tejeda,* made with coarsely ground almonds mixed with honey and lemon juice. Local honey and grated almonds are also used for little cakes called *Rapaducas,* and as in Spain, the popular almond *turron* (we call it nougat) is on sale everywhere.

We are always surprised that in places where bananas grow so prolifically they are so little used as food by the local people. They are mashed with *gofio* and milk as baby food, and the babies certainly thrive on it.

We can remember only one example of a banana dish being served to us, and that was peeled bananas cut in halves lengthwise, rolled in *gofio* and then fried in oil. This was served with squares of white cheese coated in *gofio* and fried in the same way. It was unusual, but we didn't really think it worth trying again.

But Anne frequently fried bananas in butter, then flamed them in the local Arucus rum, and this was a dish which always found favour with our neighbours when they dined with us.

And of course, there are all the usual dishes one eats in Spain, such as *paella,* that excellent mixture of rice, sea food and chicken; *gazpacho,* a delicious iced soup for summer, made with tomatoes, peppers and onions; *fritos variados,* a marvellous dish of prawns, mushrooms, artichoke hearts, and pieces of cooked chicken or fish, each separately rolled in egg and breadcrumbs and deep fried, then piled up on a plate and served with tartare sauce. Also *empanadas,* triangles of pastry filled with cooked chicken or fish, and sometimes vegetables, then carefully sealed and deep fried in oil. Sometimes *empanadas* are made with a sweet filling, such as chopped dates with honey, and fried in the same way.

Unfortunately, we usually found the Canary puddings rather sweet for our taste.

In addition to Arucas rum, a fiery spirit much beloved by the islanders – and some visitors – wine is produced in Tenerife, Grand Canary, La Palma and Lanzarote. The red wines are the best, particularly that from the lava soil of Lanzarote, but don't expect a *grand cru* here, for they are very *vin ordinaire,* but go well with the usually highly seasoned local dishes. A number of very sweet liqueurs are also produced in Arucus.

The grape vine was first introduced into Madeira in the fifteenth century and from there into the Canaries, the original plants being obtained from the famous Malmsey or Malavesi vineyards in Crete. References by Shakespeare in some of his plays to 'Canary Sack' indicate that the Canary wines were well known in England in his time. Sack was strong and sweet, a great luxury in the cold, sugarless days of the sixteenth century, a fore-runner of today's sherry. By the beginning of the nineteenth century there was a very large export trade in wine to both England and America, much of it shipped from Tenerife.

But in 1850 the vines were attacked by a fungus disease and almost exterminated. Today Tacaronte and Icod are practically the only remaining areas in Tenerife where wine is produced, and this only in limited quantities which does not even satisfy the needs of the local population.

It is interesting to see how low the vines grow here, spreading out over the ground. This is a special type of grape which absorbs the moisture from the ground into its leaves, then the sun completes the cycle which produces the Malvoisie wine, as it is called today. This grape is also grown in Lanzarote and La Palma for their wines.

Vino de Monte from Grand Canary comes from grapes trained to grow upwards in the conventional way, but in Lanzarote the vines grow in hollows in the black lava sand, which not only attracts the moisture in the air, but gives the wine its distinctive flavour.

Several types of mineral water are also produced in the islands, Firgas and La Roque being the most popular.

4. Flora and Fauna

Each of the islands of the archipelago has something different to offer the traveller, and particularly those who have an interest in plant life, whether they are professional botanists or amateur gardeners.

For here can be found valuable examples of flora which has disappeared in other countries, but which has been sustained in these islands because of climatic conditions and the circumstances which have enabled these plants to grow undisturbed for centuries. Many species regarded today as indigenous to the Canaries have been found fossilised on the shores of the Mediterranean in earth stratas dating back to the Miocene and Pliocene periods. Plants growing today in profusion on the islands have been found rightly to belong to the Tertiary period, but which by some mystery of climate and soil have survived here over the ages.

Probably the one which has always aroused the greatest interest is the Dragon Tree (*Dracaena Draco*), which naturalists claim represents the last vestiges of a prehistoric type of vegetation, and which can be found in a number of places in the islands.

The tree has a strong, fleshy trunk with long sword-like leaves growing in clusters; it grows in a rounded and fairly symmetrical shape something like a mushroom, and can reach a good height.

Extravagant claims have been made concerning the ages of various Dragon trees – the most famous one which grew at Orotava was sometimes described as being as old as the pyramids of Egypt! This tree was destroyed in a hurricane in 1867, and was so large and so old that it is claimed its hollow trunk served as a place of worship for the Guanche priests.

The largest and best known one growing today can be seen at Icod de los Vinos in Tenerife, near the church. No one knows how old that is, but its thick lower trunk has had to be strengthened with concrete in case strong winds should cause it to fall.

There is also a fine example to be seen in the garden of the Seminary, formerly the Dominican monastery, at La Laguna; and another growing by the side of the road at Tacaronte. Several smaller ones can be seen in the grounds of the Hotel Santa Catalina in Las Palmas.

Since the government wisely declared these trees as being officially protected, many small ones have been able to grow unscathed. There was even one growing on the footpath beside the main road in Puerto just outside the Belair apartments where we stayed on our last visit, and many others can be seen throughout the archipelago, but these are comparative youngsters in age.

The sap of the dragon tree is dark red like coagulated blood – dragon's blood it is called – and the tree must have been known in Europe at some early time, for Dante wrote of the tree which dripped blood, and in the early Middle Ages dragon's blood was claimed to be a cure for leprosy.

The Guanches used this sap as an ingredient for mummifying their chiefs, and it was probably also used as a dye by those who made the cloaks worn by the chiefs and their wives.

But the dragon tree is not the only remaining plant from prehistoric times, and the desert-growing euphorbia, of which there are several kinds growing in the islands, certainly looks as if it comes from another era. This plant has the facility of growing in the old lava flows, but care should be taken in handling it as the sap is poisonous. It is said that the Guanches poured the juice of the euphorbia on the water when fishing. This stupefied the fish without poisoning them, thus making it easier to catch them.

3 (*opposite*) *The bronze dogs guarding the Plaza Santa Ana, Las Palmas.*

The desert country also supports prickly pear (Opuntia) and Sempervivum in abundance. Many sisal plants can be seen as dividing fences for fields, and in some places in plantations for the making of a form of hemp. They are also used as cattle feed when other feed is in short supply.

A special type of broom (Cytisus) which grows only at altitudes of from 6,000 to 8,000 feet is found in Las Cañadas in Tenerife, and is one of the most striking plants of the islands.

At the end of April a profusion of highly scented blossoms covers the stiff twigs of the Retama de Pico, as it is known, growing from beneath the shadow of the mighty Teide, from seemingly arid soil covered with rocks, the flowers presenting a splendid sight for just a brief period.

Another plant which blossoms beneath Teide's mountain peak is the Viper's Bugloss, known here as the Pride of Tenerife, and several good examples of this can be seen growing near the Parador at Las Cañadas. It rises up to seven feet in height in an elongated pyramid shape, covered in tiny rose-red flowers, looking most attractive.

But those who laboriously climb Teide's slopes will find another flower unique to this area, the so-called 'Violet of the Teide', a species of viola growing only at an altitude of over 9000 feet. This little flower, pale blue-violet in colour, is the only vegetation which reaches the upper heights of the mountain, braving the strong winds and the sulphurous fumes coming from the mouths of the fumaroles or craters surrounding El Pico.

When the famous naturalist and explorer, Baron Alexander von Humboldt, visited the Canary Islands on his way to South America in 1799, he investigated the geology and botany of the islands, and likened them to the fabled Gardens of the Hesperides of which Plato wrote.

He was particularly impressed with the fertile Orotava Valley, which looked very different in his time to the valley filled with banana plantations we see today. Before the new highway was built between Santa Cruz and Puerto there was a corner of the old road known as Humboldt's Corner, and it was from here that he was supposed to have had his first view

4 *(opposite) Courtyard and well in Casa de Colon.*

of the verdant valley he considered the most beautiful on earth.

Today's visitors may not entirely agree with him about this valley, but they will find a colourful display of tropical and sub-tropical plants all over the archipelago wherever there is water.

Houses and walls are covered in red, purple and orange bougainvillea and delicate blue thunbergia. Fuchsias, hibiscus and oleanders grow as large as trees, as also do the flaming red poinsettias and the daturas with their white trumpets in full bloom which fill the night air with their heavy perfume. Geraniums, especially the climbing variety, grow like weeds and hang down over fences and balconies in pink and red profusion.

And everywhere there are bananas with their large leaves and exotic purple flowers which become fingers of golden sweetness. Bananas which are the life-blood of the Canary economy, along with tomatoes – and tourists.

Bananas grow on irrigable land up to an altitude of about 800 feet, usually in terraces, and land planted with bananas takes about 18 months to come into production, the plants continuing to bear fruit for many years. The banana most common in the Canaries is the Chinese variety (*Musa Cavendishii*), rather smaller than the West Indian species, but sweet and very good to eat. Strangely, the Canarios do not seem to eat many bananas – perhaps they see so many of them growing that there is no attraction except as a marketable product.

We lived for some time beside a plantation, and it was fascinating to watch the progress of growth of these strange plants, with their purple-sheathed flowers hanging down in bunches or *racimos*. Each trunk produces only one bunch of flowers, which vary in size, each flower becoming a separate banana. The bunches of fruit are harvested green, which allows them to ripen slowly during the voyage to England or one of the Continental ports. A bunch or stem of bananas averages from 55 to 65 pounds, although much larger ones are found.

After harvesting the fruit the old trunk is cut down, then gradually suckers make their appearance round the old trunk. These suckers are usually reduced to three, which come on in succession, producing in turn their flowers and fruit.

Living beside a plantation can be a noisy business at times, for the large papery leaves sway about and slap into each other, and are often torn to shreds when the wind blows, but one gets accustomed to it in time.

But bananas are not the only fruit one sees growing in profusion here. There are avocado and papaya (paw-paw) trees in almost every garden; oranges and lemons bear heavy, juicy fruit at the same time as their fragrant blossoms, and apricots, almonds and walnuts grow well in some areas.

In the hills are forests of chestnuts and the distinctive Canario laurels and pine trees. These forests are not as thick as they once were, for many trees were cut down by the charcoal-burners in the eighteenth and nineteenth centuries. Goats and rabbits also took their toll of the lower vegetation, resulting in erosion on the bare slopes, but all over the islands the government is planting new forests of Canary pines to combat this erosion as well as for timber, but more importantly, for encouraging water condensation from the low trade-wind clouds.

As only about one-third of the present flora growing in the islands is really indigenous, many trees and flowers from other lands which now flourish in the islands are familiar to visitors.

Australian eucalypts (which sometimes made us feel very home-sick) grow prodigiously in this climate, and scent the air as one drives on roads lined with these large rough-barked trees, of which many varieties are grown in the archipelago. One sees date palms and sugar cane, tobacco and corn, coffee beans, potatoes and grapevines – the latter growing low on the ground instead of climbing over wires as we are more accustomed to seeing them.

Roses and carnations are grown under the cover of plastic frames to keep their beauty untouched for export to Europe during the winter months. Cucumbers are also grown under plastic for the export market, and very good they are, too.

For those who would like to make a closer study of the flora of the islands there is a Jardin Botanico on both Tenerife and Grand Canary. The latter is at Tafira on the way to Santa Brigida, and here only plants indigenous to the islands are grown. The former is on the outskirts of Puerto, and was first established as an acclimatization garden for plants from Central and South America which were to be taken to Madrid for their botanical gardens. Today within its small area can be seen examples of every kind of flora which grows in the archipelago, whether indigenous or foreign. This garden could be of great interest to those who like to grow exotic plants, particularly cacti and succulents, of which there are many examples, and unusual house plants.

As with the case of the flora of the islands, strange survivals are also apparent in the fauna, notably the giant lizards which live only on the Roque de Anaga and the Roques de Salmor in the island of Hierro. Fossilised remains of giant land tortoises, enormous snails and large rodents have been found, showing that these lived in the archipelago before the advent of man.

There are, of course, many examples of Canary dogs after which the islands are named, but over the years these have been so cross-bred with other types it is almost impossible to recognise any particular species, although Fuerteventura does have it *bardinos*.

There are no wild or harmful animals, and no snakes, and throughout the islands one only finds small rodents and many small lizards basking in the sun – perhaps descendants of those earlier giants. The many rabbits provide good meals for the country folk.

Birds are numerous, from the brownish-coloured wild canary – which takes it name from the islands and not vice-versa as most people believe – through a variety of ring-doves, owls, falcons and sparrow-hawks, swallows, swifts and the beautifully plumaged hoopoes, as well as numerous sea birds.

High in the rugged crests of the mountains can be found the small Canary eagle, and down in the valleys are the game birds of the islands, widgeons, quails and partridges.

And just as Teide nurtures one special flower on its heights, so does it offer a home to only one species of bird, known as the Bird of Teide (*Fringilla Tedea*), a rather drab, stone-coloured little bird which gracefully swoops and glides round the mighty peak, defying the winds which blow here. Like the flower of Teide, it looks too delicate to withstand the heights at this altitude, but both bird and flower only add a little more to the mystery of these islands.

From the point of view of both entomologists and botanists this archipelago offers rewarding scope to investigators in both fields.

5. Grand Canary

Often called a continent in miniature because of the great variety of scenery and climate contained within its 538 square miles, the island of Grand Canary has the shape of a scallop shell turned upside-down. Its highest point, Pozo de las Nieves, 6,400 feet, is roughly in the centre of the island, and the sides of the 'shell' are furrowed with long, deep ravines or *barrancos*.

The interior of the island is generally green and very fertile wherever there is water, and the building of many reservoirs in the mountains has helped the farmers increase their crops of both bananas and tomatoes.

Approaching the capital, Las Palmas, by ship one sees a long line of continuous development extending from the bare hilly peninsula of La Isleta at the north-east corner of the port, for some five miles along the eastern coast.

Multi-storey apartment buildings climb up the bare hills backing the coastal strip, and more and more skyscraper office blocks and hotels rise above the twin towers of the Cathedral in the old part of the city, known as the Vegueta.

It was here by the Guiniguada barranco that the Spanish invaders under Juan Rejón built their stockade against the Guanches, using the tall straight palms which grew so prolifically by the old river bed. And it was these that gave the future city its name, La Ciudad de Las Palmas de Gran Canaria, as it is officially – the City of the Palms of Grand Canary.

Rejón and his forces had made a landing at Gando, site of

the present airport, in June 1478 – that is a matter of history, but here we come to one of those legends so dear to the Canarios.

The Spanish were preparing to march southwards, when from a thicket a withered crone appeared to Rejón and advised him against the project because of the distance and because the Guanches were very hostile. Instead, she told him, go in the opposite direction until you come to a spot where the palm trees are so plentiful they shut out the view of the sky. The old woman then disappeared as mysteriously as she had come, but Rejón decided to take her advice, telling his men that she was Santa Ana herself, come to assist them in their struggle against the non-believers.

They found the forest of palm trees, and here the bloody battle of Guiniguada was fought, with the ultimate victory going to the Spaniards, partly due to the terror of the Guanches at seeing horses for the first time. But the long struggle for Grand Canary was not to be finalised for another five years, when Pedro de Vera who succeeded Rejón as commander of the Spanish forces, completed the conquest of the island.

An important milestone in the ultimate victory was the capture of Thenesor Semidan, the chief or Guanarteme, who after several battles and realising the might of the invaders, became reconciled to the prospect of Spanish domination as a way of saving his people. With the idea of using this as a form of propaganda, he was taken to Spain and presented to the king.

He became converted to Christianity and was baptised as Fernando Guanarteme, and then returned to Grand Canary to persuade his people to surrender to the Spaniards – accompanied by five shiploads of soldiers to assist in his persuasion.

But the Guanches were not to give in without one more struggle for their freedom, and they waged a series of fairly successful guerilla skirmishes in the mountains against the invaders. Undaunted, de Vera reorganised his forces and soon had the Guanche warriors hemmed in and at the mercy of the strongly armed Spaniards.

It was then that Guanarteme at last convinced the majority of the aborigines of the futility of further resistance, and he induced them to surrender on promise of good treatment. But the Guanche leader, Bentejui, and his second-in-command refused this humiliation and they committed suicide by throwing themselves over a high cliff.

Acceptance of Christianity and the sovereignty of the king of Spain were the only conditions imposed by the victors, and the formal capitulation took place on 29 April 1483, just five years after Juan Rejón's victory at Guiniguada.

Las Palmas developed fairly rapidly into an important settlement, and records show that in 1492 Columbus called there to find sailmakers and carpenters, as well as water and provisions, on his way to the New World, and made subsequent visits on his next voyages.

As Spain and England were bitter enemies during the sixteenth and seventeenth centuries it is not surprising that the islands – being a Spanish possession – were several times attacked by English ships, but with little success.

Drake and Hawkins, with a substantial fleet, attacked Las Palmas in 1595, but found it too well defended and withdrew.

The Dutch Admiral Van der Does and his ships were more successful in 1599, and occupied the city for some days, causing some damage, but they were soon driven away. Several other English naval forces visited Las Palmas over the years but did no harm.

In addition to these attacks, Moorish slave traders and privateers of many nations also raided the island.

But these were not the only enemies from which Grand Canary suffered, for plagues of yellow fever and cholera in the nineteenth century decimated the population, almost halving it.

In September 1927, the archipelago was divided into two provinces, and Fuerteventura and Lanzarote joined with Grand Canary as the eastern province, with Las Palmas as the capital and seat of government.

First a few words about Puerto de la Luz, the port of arrival for all those coming to Grand Canary by sea.

And here we have another legend to add to those already mentioned. It is said that a party of sailors, possibly from Majorca, who made frequent trips to the islands in the early days, built a little chapel or hermitage near La Isleta. One night a mysterious light appeared over the mountain peaks and descended towards the sea, hovering over the chapel before disappearing.

This was repeated several times, until the awed and curious natives looked through a crack in the wall of the little shrine and saw a great light resting above the statue of the Virgin, filling the building with 'a glorious splendour'.

And so the port became Puerto de la Luz, or Port of Light, and it is still called that today.

The Mallorquin sailors also bequeathed another of their names to the island, that of their patron saint, Catherine, or Santa Catalina, and we will find this used for several places, notably Santa Catalina Park, not far from the port area.

Usually ships tie up alongside one of the quays, making disembarkation very simple, and from there you can take a taxi into town – or you can walk if you feel energetic and have no luggage to carry. This is a free port, so there are no customs and few passport regulations.

Occasionally, as once happened to us when we arrived here on the *Oriana* en route to South Africa, the ship is anchored outside and you are transported in by launch, which makes a pleasant change.

This is a very busy port, once a coal-bunkering station for ships travelling to South America, South and West Africa, and now just as important for taking on oil supplies; not because it has any oil wells but because its refineries are kept supplied by the big tankers which call here. It is claimed Las Palmas handles the largest gross tonnage of any Spanish port.

The newest quay (or *muelle,* as they call it here), the Santa Catalina, was planned by Don Juan de Leon y Castillo, an impressive name you will meet again in the long street which starts from the Santa Catalina quay, borders the shore line for a time, then takes you right into the heart of the city, where it becomes Calle Triana, the main shopping street. (*Calle* means street in Spanish.)

The moated and towered grey stone Castillo de la Luz, built in 1492 to guard the port, has recently been restored and given a new lease of life as a museum.

After leaving the immediate shipping area you come to the busy Calle Albareda, a street of little shops, the majority owned by Indians who have settled in the islands as traders, and as always, they are hard bargainers. Here you will find cameras and transistor radios, tape recorders, electric shavers and binoculars, pocket calculators and walkie-talkies, as well as souvenirs of all kinds.

When we first came to the islands all these goods were amazingly cheap in comparison to British and European prices, but now the Spanish government has placed a heavy tax on all imported goods, and bargains are not so easy to find, except in cigarettes, tobacco and liquor.

But as with shopping in all foreign ports one has to be sure of customs regulations at home before making extensive purchases.

This is the narrowest part of the isthmus which joins La Isleta to the main part of the island. La Isleta was a Guanche burial ground, and a quarry here provided much of the building stone used in Las Palmas, but because of military installations on much of the islet, it is not possible to come here without a permit.

On the other side of the isthmus is the half-moon beach of Las Canteras, throughout the year the favourite spot of tourists. It is a pleasant beach, protected over its entire length by natural reefs, which make it very safe for swimming.

In this area many of the main hotels are to be found, most of them built in the last ten years, and very comfortable with good restaurants. The larger ones such as the Reina Isabel and the Cristina even have swimming pools for those who like to be beside the sea but not venture into it.

There is a long tiled promenade bordering the beach, a favourite place for the old Spanish custom of the *paseo,* where the local boys and girls stroll up and down in the evenings.

Here are restaurants and snack bars of all kinds, catering for Germans (pickled herrings) and Danes (smørrebrød), English (fish and chips) and Americans (hamburgers), and even for the Spanish (*calamares*). There are also quite a number of night clubs, some expensive with good floor shows, others sleazy and noisy; as well as several discotheques.

This was largely a working-class residential district, with small shops and bars, before the great influx of tourists and the necessity for building large hotels to accommodate them. It was here by the sea that we had our small apartment when we first came to stay in Las Palmas.

Today a great many of the little shops have been transformed into smart boutiques, and the bars have been tarted-up for the tourists, but most of these are run by foreigners, not by the locals who are gradually being pushed out of this district and up into the new government-built apartments in the hills above the town.

It is in this district, at Sagasta 5, that you will find the British American Clinic, staffed by British doctors, and with a 24-hour emergency service, a piece of information which could be useful for visitors of all nationalities.

From here it is only a short walk back to Albareda where we started our exploration of Las Palmas. Albareda leads directly into the Parque Santa Catalina, which is not really a park as we know the word, but rather a large paved square, with tables set out beneath the shade of palms and enormous Canary laurel trees, and well-stocked stalls where you can buy everything from a postcard to a zebra-skin rug.

This is a favourite rendezvous for foreign residents and tourists alike; international newspapers are on sale here and you can sit in the shade with a cool beer at your elbow and catch up with the latest gossip and the world's news.

Just opposite the Parque is another tree-shaded square where the itinerant artists gather with their easels and paints, and here you can have your portrait painted while you sit patiently in full view of the passing crowd.

Highly colourful paintings are hung from canvas screens around the square while the hopeful artists wait for somebody to buy – and it is surprising how many sales they do make.

Adjoining this outdoor exhibition is a most attractive two-storied house, designed in the Canario style by the famous island artist, Nestor de la Torre, of whom we will hear more later. This is the Las Palmas tourist office, and here the helpful staff can answer your questions about the city and the island, plan excursions and recommend hotels and restaurants, hairdressers and dentists, as need be. Here, too, can be found brochures and books on the island in English, French, German and Spanish.

At the entrance to the Santa Catalina quay, just across from the tourist office, are to be found the shipping offices where passage arrangements can be made for the inter-island steamers.

The journey from here into the centre of the city can be made by frequent bus services. This bus takes you past the Playa de las Alcaravaneras, a beach where there are always plenty of local children playing on the sands, but few tourists, for the waters of the port are not so inviting as those of the Canteras beach on the other side of the isthmus.

Let us continue on into the city, through the exclusive residential section known as the Ciudad Jardin, or Garden City. Here there are all types of architecture, from the stone Canario houses to those of the second Empire, or even early Victorian mansions. Gardens blaze with the colours of bougainvillea, hibiscus, strelitzia and ivy geraniums, and all the sun-loving flowers you can imagine.

The British Club and the British church, both open to visitors, are situated in this district. The Club, which was founded in 1908, and adjoins the Hotel Metropole, has a library, a bar and restaurant, facilities for billiards and bridge, and is the setting for social gatherings, dances, a drama group and debates, and the members are always pleased to see new faces.

The Ciudad Jardin extends from Leon y Castillo through to Paseo de Chil, the wide road at the base of the foothills, and for those staying in Las Palmas a walk through here is very rewarding.

Not far beyond here, situated about half-way betwen the Parque Santa Catalina and the city proper, one comes to what we consider the loveliest hotel in the islands, the Santa Catalina, placed against the background of the Parque Doramas (another Guanche name), fifteen acres of lush garden containing swimming pool, tennis courts and bowling green. This hotel is a splended example of Canario architecture, showing all the skills of good craftsmen in the exterior carved wooden balconies, and interior mosaics and painted murals.

Not a new hotel, it has been cleverly modernised without spoiling its graciousness, and we have always found the food here as good as the hotel design.

In the same gardens, adjoining the hotel, is another example of Canario architecture, the Pueblo Canario. Designed by Nestor to typify the perfect Canary village, it is built round a large plaza, as if round a village square.

Here is the stone building of the Nestor museum, with a splendid permanent exhibition of his paintings – you may think his style is rather dated, but his use of colour is magnificent, and his paintings of local plant life are delightful. There is a portrait here showing a young woman who is the image of Liza Minelli.

Adjoining the museum is another building with an information office and a tiny chapel, and at the other end of the plaza is a restaurant, with a bar serving drinks outside in the shade of umbrellas. On the other side of the plaza is a splended example of Canario balconies, and here on two floors are shops selling all the best of the island's handicraft. Even if you are not looking for souvenirs to buy, go upstairs and see the Canario costumes displayed here from all the islands.

But the best time to see such costumes is when they are worn by the troupe of folk dancers who perform here on Sunday mornings and Thursday evenings. It is a charming and very colourful sight, the girls in long full skirts in various colours and patterns, over which is worn a looped-up overskirt in pastel cotton heavily embroidered with drawn-thread work, known as *calados,* and a speciality of Canario women. Their tight white bodices are also embroidered, and their little black hats are perched over head scarves to match their over-skirts, a costume designed to make these pretty girls even more attractive.

The men wear costumes somewhat reminiscent of those of the Greek islanders, full white cotton knee-length pants, full-sleeved white shirts and coloured waistcoats.

They all dance with great verve and style to the music of guitars and timples, the latter a five-stringed instrument resembling a small mandolin, and found only in these islands. There are the stirring rhythms of the 'Saltona' and the 'Tajaraste', the gay 'Isa', and the sad 'Folio', all traditional tunes which can be heard not only at the Pueblo Canario but also at fiestas, pilgrimages and weddings in country villages, when the charming folk costumes are still worn.

Pueblo Canario is an appropriate setting for the gay dancers and music of the island, and passengers from cruise ships staying only a brief while in Las Palmas are brought here for a glimpse of Canary art and architecture, costume and crafts. It is the island in miniature, to be seen and enjoyed in an hour.

The Canarios are very proud of their artists, writers and poets, especially in Las Palmas, where they honour them with statues and name streets and plazas after them. The fact that few of these intellectuals are known outside the islands does not bother their admirers – it is enough that they have gained fame in their own city, a case of honour in his own country.

Nestor de la Torre, designer of both the Pueblo Canario and the tourist office opposite the Parque Catalina, also decorated the very impressive Galdos theatre down by the Guiniguada barranco at the end of Triana, where concerts and plays (in Spanish) are presented. The theatre has a splendid carved staircase leading to the Saint Saens hall with its murals of Canario fruit and flowers. The composer Saint Saens lived for a time in Las Palmas and wrote some important works here.

This theatre is called after the Canario novelist, Benito Perez Galdos, and there is also a very striking statue of Galdos in the Plaza de la Feria, the work of a fellow countryman,

Pablo Serrano. Galdos is further honoured in his village birthplace, Cano, where his house has been made into a museum to his memory.

Opposite the Santa Catalina Hotel a small public garden is named for the poet, Alonso Quesada, and another poet, Tomas Morales, known as the 'Singer of the Sea', not only has a plaza but also a street named for him, as well as a statue to show what he looked like.

Another square, an oasis of green in the midst of the busy city traffic is the Plaza Cairasco, called after a poet, Bartolomé Cayrasco de Figueroa who was born on the island in 1540. He wrote many allegorical poems about the Guanches, and it is rather appropriate that the Gabinete Literario, the exclusive literary club of Las Palmas, should overlook the little square. There is also a collection of shaded tables and chairs here where tired sightseers can sit and enjoy a cool drink brought over from the neighbouring bar.

For one of the most pleasant panoramic views of Las Palmas we must return to the Parque Doramas and the Santa Catalina Hotel, but instead of entering the hotel, walk towards the back through the gardens until you reach the Paseo de Chil, a wide busy boulevard.

Cross over here (use the marked crossing) and mount the steps which go up the hill in three flights until you reach the half-moon of the look-out. The view is well worth the climb, and if you need refreshment after all those steps there is a very pleasant bar-restaurant here set in a pleasant garden.

The Paseo de Chil extends right across the city just below the foothills, and is named after the man who made this fine road possible. Dr Gregorio Chil was an historian who was responsible for founding the Museo Canario, with its excellent collection of Guanche relics, but he will probably be remembered more for his road than his museum.

In 1879 when the crops failed disastrously in Lanzarote and Fuerteventura, many of the starving people fled to Grand Canary looking for work and sustenance. To provide them with employment Dr Chil organised a relief fund and set them to work building the road in return for a livelihood. His memory is certainly blessed by all those motorists who travel across the city each day on his splended boulevard.

In the heights above the city are the modern housing estates of Escaleritas and Schamann, block after towering block of government-built *casas baratas,* providing cheap accommodation for the ever-growing population. Gua-guas transport the residents up the hilly roads each night after their work in the city or the docks, and up here, no matter how hot it is in the old part of the city, there is always a fresh breeze.

The Paseo de Chil is not the only fine boulevard extending through the city, for along the sea front is the Avenida Maritima, which runs from the Playa de las Alcaravaneras to join up with the highway going to the south of the island.

This is not just a fine road, it is also a fine engineering feat, for this road and the land adjoining it were reclaimed from the sea during the last ten years, providing a new frontage on the waterfront which was soon claimed by the property developers for new hotels, apartments, and office blocks.

For a section of the way a monorail has been built, but unfortunately this grandiose scheme is not likely to provide extra transport facilities for the people of Las Palmas, for the city authorities have decided not to go ahead with the original plan of linking the city with the airport by means of this overhead railway. It was even rumoured during our last visit that the whole business was to be pulled down, which seems a pity, for at least the present section could be a novel tourist attraction – or at least provide the children with some exciting rides.

Some way along the Avenida is another very ambitious landmark which has not quite fulfilled the expectations of its effectiveness. This is a large fountain which was built to typify Las Palmas, for it offers colour, music and water all together. It is supposed to play every Sunday and for all fiestas and special occasions but we only once saw it in action. It has 33 water jets and is illuminated in three colour ranges, and while the spectacular display of coloured water is going on, suitable music is broadcast as an accompaniment.

For those looking for the main shopping district, the street to find is Triana, which is really a continuation of Leon y Castillo, that long street which extends from the Parque Santa Catalina.

But at the beginning of Triana you come to another of those pleasant paved squares, shaded by palms and Canary laurels, and with tables and chairs where cool drinks can be enjoyed. This is Parque San Telmo, and after you have had your drink go and look at the quaint little chapel heavily overshadowed by giant trees at the corner of the square.

Built in the eighteenth century in honour of San Telmo, patron saint of the island's fishermen, the little chapel is usually open mornings and evenings. The statue of the saint is finely carved, and there is an interesting monstrance showing a pelican holding the sun on its head.

Opposite San Telmo, on the walls of the office of the Military Governor, can be seen a plaque commemorating the National Rising which Franco planned in the Canary Islands, and which culminated in the tragic Spanish Civil War.

Postpone your shopping for another time; after all, today there is very little difference in the merchandise of Las Palmas, Liverpool or Luxembourg, and come across the Barranco de Guiniguada – scene of the bloody battle between the Guanches and the Spanish invaders mentioned earlier – to the ancient streets of the original part of the city.

This is Vegueta, for centuries the aristocratic section of Las Palmas, as can be seen by the splendid doorways surmounted by coats-of-arms leading to many of the old houses. Unfortunately the constant stream of traffic, and the closely parked cars along the narrow streets, makes it difficult to see these charming old houses to the best advantage. It is a pity that the city authorities could not declare at least some of this picturesque and historic quarter free of traffic during the day – we are sure the tourists would appreciate it, as well as those who live here.

Central point of this ancient section is the Cathedral of Santa Ana (remember the withered crone who appeared to Juan Rejón), and facing it across the Plaza Santa Ana is the impressive facade of the Ayuntiamento or Town Hall. The entrance to the plaza is guarded by the statues of eight bronze dogs, reminders of the fierce dogs which are claimed to have given the archipelago its name. The originals may have been fierce, but their replicas are much appreciated by the small children of Las Palmas, who love to ride on their smooth backs.

The Cathedral is an extraordinary mixture of architecture, predominantly Gothic, and the work of a number of planners, for it was started in 1497 and completed in 1791. There is a story that the workmen compelled the last architect to stand beneath the dome as they completed the large curve, as they had no confidence that it would hold up. Time has fortunately proved them wrong.

In addition to the dome it has two towers, both added at different times, and not even the windows match, but it is quite an imposing building, if rather gloomy.

Go through to the Treasury (there is a sign pointing the way, and a custodian will sell you a ticket for a few pesetas) and see the pyx in gold and enamel attributed to Benvenuto Cellini; a golden chalice ornamented with emeralds given to the cathedral by Philip IV of Spain; a baroque lamp made in Genoa to the order of the island's wealthy sugar and wine exporters; some beautiful silverwork by local silversmiths, and some of the altar plate from St Paul's Cathedral, London, which was sold during the sacking of the churches under Oliver Cromwell.

There are colourful banners and ecclesiastical robes heavily embroidered in silver and gold thread, massive silver altar plate and many other items of interest, but the whole collection is displayed in rather dusty-looking cases, poorly lit and with an air of neglect over everything, which is a pity for there are some interesting and beautiful things there.

At the rear of the cathedral, in the Calle Colon, is the Casa de Colon or Columbus' House, a building whose recently restored interior is as interesting as its exterior. It has an impressive stone-framed doorway and those typical Canario balconies in carved wood which surely owe their inspiration to the centuries of Moorish occupation of the mother country.

This house never belonged to Columbus, but to the early Governors of the island, and the explorer was a guest here during his three visits to Las Palmas en route to the New World.

The Canary Islands were a useful stepping-stone between Europe and the New World for ships to be re-stocked with food and water, and any necessary repairs to be carried out. It is claimed that it was Canary sugar cane which was planted in the West Indies by Columbus' men, and from which came the later prosperity of those islands.

One of the early Governors of Las Palmas, Antonio de Torres, was such a good friend of the explorer that he accompanied him on his second journey.

The old house, which has been much restored and rebuilt over the centuries, is now a museum with mementoes of Columbus mixed with relics from the days of the conquest of the islands, and some early paintings sent from the Prado collection in Madrid.

There are twin patios inside the house, the first one with a small bubbling fountain and an abundance of green plants giving an appearance of fresh coolness on the warmest days. Canaries – those little yellow birds which took their name from the islands – sing shrilly in bamboo cages, and bright-coloured parrots squawk among the greenery. On the plaster walls beneath the carved wooden gallery are drawn maps showing the voyages of Columbus, and there are many letters and documents pertaining to these voyages stored away in the archives, along with official documents dealing with the early days of the Spanish settlement.

Among the many paintings is one which is claimed to portray Columbus with his little son, Diego.

The rooms are spacious, with splendid ceilings of carved wood, inspired like the Canario balconies, by the Moorish craftsmen in Spain, but here carried out by skilled Canario artisans.

The second patio is centred by an old stone-framed well, from which sweet water can still be drawn up as it was in the explorer's day, and our guide assured us that this was the well from which Columbus drank during his stay here. The magnificent stone-framed doorway leading from this patio is worthy of notice. Down in the crypt is a secret (?) passage leading to the cathedral, through which the governor could escape if the need should arise.

The little church of San Antonio Abad, at the back of the Casa de Colon, and known as Columbus' Church, is worth visiting after leaving the governors' house, but you will be lucky to find it open – we never have. It was not built until 1796, so was certainly not known to Columbus, but it was erected on the ruins of the first church to be built on the island, and undoubtedly it was in the early church that he attended mass on his visits to Las Palmas.

An American friend of ours, an amateur historian, who was spending his first holiday on the island told us the discovery of these links between the explorer and the islands had made all the difference to his holiday. To find so much interest and pride here in Columbus, and being able to see the buildings connected with him, made him decide to come back again and buy a small villa where he could retire and devote himself to his hobby.

This he did, but unfortunately he had a heart attack and died some time later – but not before he had visited Gomera and investigated that island's connections with Christobel Colon – whom we call Christopher Columbus.

There are other splendid old houses in Vegueta, many notable for their impressive stone-framed doorways and wooden balconies, and the best way to find these is to walk through the narrow streets around the cathedral. In Calle Leon y Joven you will find a group of houses, all with heraldic devices over their entrances, and if the doors should be ajar you would see the charming patios around which the rooms are built.

One of the most magnificent examples of these stone-framed entrances is that of the Seminary in Calle Dr Chil, with its twisted pillars on each side. Further up this street (named for the Dr Chil we have already mentioned in connection with the boulevard) is the Canario museum, which contains what is claimed to be the most extensive collection of Gaunche relics. (Tenerife makes the same claim for its Archaeological Museum.)

The nucleus of this collection had been made by Dr Chil, who bequeathed it and his spacious house to the city for a museum. For those interested in the early inhabitants of the islands this is a fascinating assortment of objects relating to these almost prehistoric people.

Two churches in this district are of interest – San Francisco and Santo Domingo. Both were damaged during the Dutch invasion of Las Palmas during the sixteenth century and reconstructed at a later date.

The church of San Francisco, in a corner of the square leading from the Plaza Cairasco, is the favourite of the people of the city, and the choice of many of the older families for weddings, christenings and funerals. Juan Rejón brought the first Franciscan friars to the island and had a monastery built here for them. It is on the site of the old monastery that the church was built in 1689.

Santo Domingo stands in the plaza of the same name right in the heart of the Vegueta, surrounded by ancient stone houses. The first cloister was built here in 1505 by Dominican monks, and many of the first Conquistadors are buried here. It was in this plaza that the peace treaty with the Guanches was finalised.

If you should be visiting Las Palmas in June over the festival of Corpus Christi, you would see the streets surrounding the cathedral covered with the flower carpets or *alfombras* for which the Canary Islands are renowned.

The Plaza Santa Ana in front of the cathedral blazes with the colours of thousands of flower petals used to create the most intricate designs, that in the plaza usually of a religious theme. The people give free rein to their artistic nature in laying down these carpets over the streets of Vegueta, and it is fascinating to watch them shape the designs with the so very delicate materials they are using.

All join in; schoolchildren have their own section just as do members of the forces, while many families lay their own flower carpets in front of their houses.

An hour before dusk the carpets are completed; the side-walks are crowded with people moving slowly along the carpeted route, pausing to admire each design and congratulate the artists. Dogs and cats are kept locked up in case they stray on to these lovingly made works of floral art.

Then at six o'clock the bells of the cathedral ring out, the massive doors open and a procession of city officials, military, naval and air force officers and church dignitaries precede the bishop – a magnificent figure in rich cope and mitre. Then comes the huge monstrance, richly decorated, and carried by a dozen men.

For two hours the procession winds through the flower-carpeted streets, crushing the blooms beneath their feet, and then turns into the plaza. The bishop and the mayor mount the steps into the town hall and reappear on the balcony overlooking the plaza, now packed with people. A blaze of lights comes on and flower petals rain down from the roof on to the bishop as he raises his hand to bless the people.

It is a scene of dramatic beauty, solemn and impressive, dissolving in a minute as the bishop disappears indoors, and the children break the tension by pelting each other with the crushed petals. The crowd disperses, leaving only the street-sweepers to get on with their work of clearing up.

(For a more detailed description of the making and history of these flower carpets see pages 00–00 on La Orotava.)

Grand Canary is not a large island; it measures 34 miles from north to south and 29 miles from east to west. Because of its mountains and fertile valleys and the deep *barrancos* which reach in many cases from the centre of the island to the coast, there are few straight roads and distances from one point to another are much longer than would appear on a map.

There are three main routes for exploring the island, north, centre and south, and these are covered by coach excursions arranged by various travel agencies, with multilingual guides. Lunch is included on these tours, usually for an extra charge, but if you are staying at a hotel with full pension it is sometimes a good idea to ask for a packed lunch, for there are always pleasant parks or tree-shaded plazas with seats where you can have a simple picnic. This also gives you extra time to wander about the town where the coach has stopped, probably allowing you to see much more than those passengers sitting indoors over a large meal.

For those who have hired self-drive cars for their stay, maps and information about various routes are available from the tourist office opposite the Parque Santa Catalina. For a party of three or four people taxis are a good way of touring, and a number of the drivers speak reasonable English and are excellent guides. One of our favourite taxi drivers was Eugenio, usually to be found on the taxi rank at the Santa Catalina Hotel.

Many of the most interesting towns can be reached by the ordinary buses (the bus station for both north and south routes is at the back of the Parque San Telmo), but make sure before leaving that you can get a return bus on the same day, as some places only have an irregular service.

We have used these ordinary buses many times, and found them a good way of meeting the country people, but as they are usually very crowded get to the bus station in plenty of time or you may not get a seat.

Again, the tourist office is the best place to make inquiries about these buses – we have found that hotels rarely know about such things – or say they don't.

In describing the various routes we are not going to follow slavishly those taken by excursions, for they can change in time, but instead take you on our favourite drives, each of which can be done in a day, and each will show you different aspects of this interesting island.

The northern route from Las Palmas can go inland through the fertile banana lands of Tamaraceite and Tenoya to Arucus, or you can follow the coast road to Banaderos and then on to Arucus. This historic town, second in size to Las Palmas, is known as the capital of the island's banana zone, and the many elegant homes here indicate the prosperity of the plantation owners. Sugar has for long also been an important crop here, and there is a large rum distillery on the outskirts of the town where a somewhat fiery rum is produced. This is very popular among the islanders, as are the various fruit liqueurs also made here, but we found these too sweet for our taste. Visitors are usually welcomed here.

Some distance before reaching Arucus you will see the triple towers of the church above the surrounding houses. Comparatively modern (it was built in the nineteenth century), it has the appearance of having been here for centuries, and is much loved by the townspeople. Built of grey granite in a very ornate Gothic style, somewhat reminiscent of French architecture, it is well proportioned inside with some interesting stone work.

Drive up Monte de Arucus to the mirador, and if it is a clear day you will have a fine view of Tenerife and its landmark, Teide. From here, too, you will see why Arucus is the capital of the banana districts, but even more interesting are the glistening waters of the reservoirs which contrast with the green of the plantations, for without these reservoirs there would be no bananas.

For water is the life-blood of the island, and distribution of water is bought by the hour in regulated volume for purposes of irrigation. Many new reservoirs have been built, mainly on a co-operative basis by growers, or sometimes by private enterprise as an investment. Water is a form of wealth on these islands, and a man who has a well on his land is indeed fortunate.

But let us continue with our tour for we have a long way to travel. From Arucus we will return to the coast road, and here, too, the ubiquitous bananas fill the view on the landward side, terrace after terrace of them going down to the sea, and one must admire the hard work which has gone into making these terraces.

One of the planation owners told us that the field workers make the stone terraces – there is plenty of stone here to work with – then fill each terrace with soil to one metre in depth, bringing this from the mountains. Then the little banana suckers are planted in rows. On the uppermost tiers it is necessary to enclose the plantations with high stone walls to protect them from the strong winds.

The next town on the road is Guia, but before reaching there we come to one of the most sacred places of the ancient Guanches, the Cenobio de Valerón. This is a collection of caves or grottoes, looking something like a crude honeycomb dug out of the cliff face seven stories high.

It is claimed there are more than 300 of these caves or cells, once used by the Harimaguadas, the Guanche equivalent of the Greek Vestal Virgins. You can climb to the top by a narrow path and see what may have been a meeting hall or council chamber, but if the Guanche maidens did live in these rock cells they must have been very uncomfortable, for most of the caves are very small and it is not even possible to stand upright in them.

During the Spanish invasion these caves were used as a fortress and look-out post, and from here the Guanche warriors hurled boulders and javelins down on to the invaders. Later the caves were used to store grain and some as a shelter for goats. Today they are protected as an important historical monument.

Guia is a commercial centre for the banana trade, with numbers of packing stations and warehouses here. But the centre of the little town is attractive, with tall laurels overhanging the little plaza in front of the Ayuntiamento, and a quite impressive church. Guia also has a speciality of its own, for here are manufactured the knives which every countryman carries and which have so many uses.

The handles are usually made out of cow's horns, very intricately carved and decorated, and the blade is sharp enough for the many jobs these knives are called upon to do on the farms. Similar knives are to be found in the larger souvenir shops, but if buying one be sure to choose one with a sheath, and a blade only sharp enough to cut paper, or you may be had up for carrying a lethal weapon.

Another speciality of Guia is the *Queso de Flor* made here, goats' milk cheese which is made with the addition of the thistle-like flowers of the wild artichoke, which causes the milk to curdle, and gives it the name of Flower Cheese.

A few miles further on is Galdar, near the pyramid-shaped mountain known as El Teide del Bolsillo, the pocket Teide, because like El Pico on the neighbouring island of Tenerife, its volcanic slopes are bare of vegetation. It is from this mountain that pumice stone is cut to make the pilars, or drip-stone filters still used in most country (and small town) houses all over the island. These are kept in the cool patios and water is poured through the pumice stone filter every day so that it drips slowly into a large clay vessel underneath, becoming fresh and cool in the process.

Galdar was once a fortified Guanche city, the capital of the Guanarteme or king of this area at the time of the Spanish conquest. Here he had his palace, but unfortunately this was completely demolished in the eighteenth century to make way for the building of the present church. This church has little to interest the tourist, except an ancient stone font, where it is said that all the Guanches of the court were baptised after their king had surrendered and been taken to Spain. Here he was baptised and given the name Fernando Guanarteme, and he returned to his country to find his lands divided between the conquerors, and his palace used as a Catholic church where his former subjects attended mass.

All through this area archaeologists have unearthed many important Guanche relics. The Painted Cave was discovered in 1881, with its walls decorated with a geometrical pattern worked in red and black volcanic ash, but as the ground above the cave had been planted with bananas, the dampness from the irrigation channels had almost destroyed these designs. What remains has been enclosed in a stone shelter and preserved as a National Monument but it is only open at infrequent times.

What is claimed to be the remains of a royal burial ground with some tombs are close by, and about four miles from Galdar, near Puerto de Sardina, multiple graves of the ordinary Guache people can be seen. Similar multiple graves have also been discovered at Fataga, Mogan and Moya.

There is a pleasant tree-filled plaza in front of the church, and on the other side is the unpretentious building of the

Ayuntiamento, whose sole claim to fame as far as visitors are concerned is that inside in its patio is growing a large, ancient dragon tree, looking as if the town hall had been built around it.

From Galdar we go south-west to Agaete, a town of very white houses contrasted with the brilliant colours of purple and scarlet bougainvillia and pink ivy geraniums growing over walls, and red poinsettias lining the streets. The town is centred around a large white church with red-tiled dome.

Here in August is celebrated the festival of The Branch, or La Rama, a very old fertility festival symbolised by bringing pine branches from the Tamadaba forest and submerging them in the sea to invoke the rains. Giant figures carrying branches are a feature of the procession, which is very colourful.

Not far away is the sea and the little fishing village of Puerto de las Nieves, Port of the Snows, so called because there is a clear view of Teide, so often snow-covered. On the beach here is another of the Guanche burial grounds, and rumour says that is why one never sees the local people swimming here.

When we were here last we watched the fishing boats come in with their rather meagre catches, and all the wives turn out to help their men pull the boats high up on the sand. Then the women sort out the best of the catch into baskets to be delivered to the hotels of Las Palmas; the remainder is sold on the beach to local housewives.

It is interesting to watch the fish being weighed up on an old pair of hand-held scales, with round stones from the beach as counter-weights. But nobody seems worried about the idea of short measure.

There is a small restaurant here where we had coffee and a drink, and some of the food we saw being served looked very good, particularly the fish, but we had planned to go on through the valley of Berrazales to its spa hotel for lunch.

This is a delightful valley, green and fertile, thickly planted with fruit trees, date palms and all manner of vegetables and flowers. At the top of the valley are mineral water springs, famous for the treatment of rheumatism and arthritis, and the

Hotel Guayarmina, surrounded with masses of avocado and loquat trees, geraniums and oleanders in a riot of colour, is a very well-known spa hotel.

But to our disappointment we found it closed, shutters fastened and a general air of desolation, so we went away hungry to retrace our steps back to Guia for the road to Moya and Firgas, another spa town, and from there back to Las Palmas.

From Agaete it is possible to continue south along the coast to El Risco and then on to the magnificent pine forest of Tamadaba, growing on a high plateau which can be seen from all over this side of the island. There is also a road going on to St Nicholas, but we were warned that in parts it is very dangerous, with plenty of curves in the narrow road overlooking the ocean side of the cliffs.

Looking south from Puerto de las Nieves the rocky, indented coastline is plainly visible as far as Puerto de San Nicholas. To us it appeared like a sleeping dragon stretching out into the sea, its spiny backbone the sharp peaks of the cliffs silhouetted against the sky, giving a fair indication of the rough, wild type of country of which we had been warned on this road.

We had decided that it was not for us this time, but hoped that at some future date the road will have been improved so we can explore this part of the island with its many little villages hidden among the valleys.

We have at times when driving come on to some very rough roads once the main roads are left, particularly in the mountains where land-slides are fairly common, so before venturing off main roads make careful inquiries *locally* to make sure you can get through. We say locally, for the tourist office in Las Palmas may not have been advised of any recent rough patches or road repairs on the route you have chosen.

And here it might be opportune to mention something which all too often is forgotten. In the small inland villages where tourists are still not a very usual sight it is well to remember that visitors should respect the customs of the islanders. The standards of politeness among the great majority of peasants are very high – they have a pleasant courtesy for visitors, and even if you have no common language it is surprising how a few signs can be mutually understood.

For instance, parties picnicking or eating lunch in the open should always offer something to country people who may stop nearby. It will generally be refused, but it is an old custom of the Spanish people which should be followed if possible.

You will probably find yourself being offered something in return, as we were on one occasion when we were eating our packed lunch in a quiet plaza, and a family party – probably from another village – sat down near us to eat *papas arrugadas* and cold fried fish and insisted on us having some, too. We didn't really enjoy the fish, but they seemed to appreciate the apples we gave them in return.

Our next excursion takes us into the centre of the island, with some wild rugged scenery, but full of interest. On this route you can contrast the charm of Teror, with its miraculous Virgin of the Pine and atmosphere of an old Spanish town, with the fantastic cave-villages of Artenara and Atalaya, and enjoy a very pleasant lunch up in the clouds at the Parador Nacional de Cruz de Tejeda.

We take the same route as for the northern excursion as far as Tamaraceite, then take a turning into the Teror road which leads us to one of our favourite towns.

Teror is a place where some time can be spent, for it has many attractive houses with some of the best Canario balconies on the island. The authorities here have very wisely decreed that all the old houses should be renovated in the old style, and any new buildings in the centre of the town must also conform to this design, so that sometimes it is difficult to know which houses are original and which are copies. Not that it matters, for they are all worth studying.

In the main street, near the plaza, is the House of Our Lady of the Pine, only identified by a plaque near the doorway. Now a museum, this is a most interesting example of an ancient Canario house, probably built at the end of the sixteenth century by Juan Perez de Villanueva, whose father is claimed to have founded the village of Teror. He was the first Patron of Our Lady of the Pine, and the treasures of the church were kept in this house as the residence of the Patron.

In the seventeenth century the house became the property of the noble family of Manrique de Lara, who spent their summer holidays here away from the heat of Las Palmas. The family still own the house, on which different generations have left their mark, as can be seen by the varied collection of furniture, silver and porcelain on show.

There is a delightful patio with a fountain of marble and local stone in the middle. All around are carved wooden balconies of 'tea' wood taken from the heart of Canario pines, the wood traditionally used for these balconies. All the main rooms open on to this patio, and their carved wooden ceilings are worthy of note. There is some beautiful porcelain dinner ware here, as well as other antiques to interest any collector, but also some incongruous pieces as well.

In the back courtyard are some family coaches, and two sedan chairs (complete with chamber pots under the seats) which were used to transport the ladies of the family from Las Palmas to Teror each summer. What a journey that must have been in those days of unmade roads. Another interesting relic is the four-hole W.C. in a little room off the same courtyard, each with carved backs and arms like thrones – a noble friendliness, as it were.

The legend of the Virgin of the Pine tells of some shepherds who saw a mysterious light hovering around a large pine tree. They reported this to the priest, who came and recognised the Virgin Mary standing in the tree. Then where there had been only dry ground a spring of water gushed forth. Neither the pine nor the spring remain, but a wrought iron crucifix now shows the spot.

Naturally such a miracle warranted the building of a church, dedicated to the Virgin of the Pine. The imposing building you see now was built in 1765 and is not the original church, of which only the the tower remains. The statue of the sweet-faced Virgin stands above the altar in a most impressive shrine of beaten silver; this shrine, the altar casing and the large candlesticks being the work of the renowned silversmith, Antonio Juan Correa of La Laguna, who was the maker of much of the church silver to be seen throughout the archipelago.

The church treasury here is claimed to be the richest in the islands, and we can well believe that. It is possible to inspect this by going up the stairs behind the altar, but permission must first be asked of the priest. Here you will see donations to the Virgin of gold and silver bracelets, rings and necklaces, precious jewels, a gold monstrance set with diamonds, gold plate and ornaments, as well as many be-jewelled robes for the statue, who is much revered not only in Teror but all over the island.

On 8 September each year the Fiesta del Pino is held here when the Virgin's statue is paraded with full military honours. Every town sends gifts of their best produce, pilgrims arrive from all over the archipelago, and there is a most colourful procession of floats, bands and dancing.

Leaving Teror we pass through Valleseco (dry valley) which, ironically is claimed to be the wettest spot on the island, then take the twisting, turning road to Artenara.

Just an ordinary Canary village one would think when arriving here, not hardly worth stopping to look at – until it is remembered that this is one of the famous cave-house centres of the island. But it is not until the main part of the village is left behind that the 'invisible houses' are reached.

For here no houses are to be seen, only doorways in the sides of the hills, with sometimes a small enclosed garden in front and a chimney coming out of the slope above.

This is a village of cave dwellers, people who live in caves because they want to, not because they are too poor to have a house. There is no housing shortage for these families, all they need to set up home is a pick and shovel to dig into the hillside. And some of them didn't even need to do much digging, for in this district there were numerous Guanche caves, and many of these were adapted by Canarios for their needs.

We visited a number of these cave dwellings and found them extremely comfortable. 'We are always warm in winter and cool in summer', said Señora Cirila Cubas Rodriguez, as she showed us over her home, with its four bedrooms, a large kitchen with Calor gas stove and running water, and a sitting room furnished with a glossy three-piece suite. There was a radio and TV, but unfortunately reception is very poor up in these mountains, she told us.

'But sometimes we can get a good picture and then all our neighbours crowd in to watch, for we have one of the few sets here', said she proudly.

Señora Rodriguez insisted on us tasting her home-made bread and goats' milk cheese she also makes each week, and presented us with some cuttings from the assortment of plants growing in the front patio of this cave house. Here, Señor Rodriguez had been born, as well as their four children, now attending school in one of the conventional buildings in the village.

If you should need any refreshment after your drive here, there is the La Cilla restaurant, which is worth visiting, if not for a drink, at least to look at the view. You can approach it through a tunnel cut out of the rock right through to the other side of the mountain, and there from the rock terrace you can see across the wide *barranco* to the rugged peak of El Roque Nublo, with other rocks in strange formations like crooked fingers pointing to the sky.

Sit here sipping coffee or the local rum and watch this fantastic panorama and you will understand why the Guanches worshipped these natural rock statues as gods.

But we have another mountain to climb now, that of Tejeda, where at 4756 feet a National Parador has been built amidst almost overwhelming scenery. After a ride up the wide but twisting road we arrive at the picturesque white building, and order our lunch from the extensive menu.

While it is being prepared we go out on the wide terrace and survey the mountains ranged all about us, with deep *barrancos* and tiny white villages perched on the steep slopes, and in the far distance, the sea. If it is a clear day we might see Teide,

5 *(opposite top) Vines growing in lava-sand enclosures in Lanzarote.*
6 *(opposite bottom) Market at Arrecife.*

sometimes just the peak showing above the clouds. It is a most impressive setting for such a building.

The Parador itself is very attractive, built to a design by Nestor, with curtains and chair coverings of locally woven wool fabric, and the furniture hand-carved in the heavy tea-wood. There is sleeping accommodation for 20 people in comfortable bedrooms, and this a is a very popular place for those who like to get away to the mountains for an occasional weekend.

After an excellent lunch we drive down the winding road, passing through Las Luganetas, a small village built around an attractive church, and on to San Mateo. Here, if you are interested in antiques, you should visit the small private museum established in a 300-year-old farmhouse.

The owner has gathered together the most amazing collection of old furniture, china, glass, weaving looms and old sewing machines for which any antique dealer would pay a small fortune. There is also an interesting assortment of primitive farm implements, *gofio* mills and huge pots for storing grain and oil.

Next comes Santa Brigida, green and cool, where can be found the summer homes of the wealthy families of Las Palmas. There is a good hotel here which is always popular with the English residents of the island, for they serve afternoon tea here with as much pomp and ritual as you would find at the Ritz.

From Santa Brigida you can take a side road which leads to another village of cave dwellers, La Atalaya, where the cave houses are very similar to those of Artenara. But here the caves are grouped together overlooking a *barranco* in what was formerly a Guanche stronghold, and many of these caves were almost certainly the homes of the island's aborigines before the Conquest.

Today they form the largest collection of troglodyte dwellings in the archipelago. The people seem to be very comfortable in their underground homes, most of which have a small terrace in front where they can sit outside. There are carpets on the concreted floors of these caves, and the walls

7 (*opposite top*) *Coming down from the Fire Mountains, Lanzarote.*

8 (*opposite bottom*) *Beasts of burden in Lanzarote.*

are neatly plastered. Many have electricity.

'If we need more space as our families increase we just dig into the hillside and make another room', one householder told us.

He also showed us some of the pottery made by the people of Atalaya from clay found in the vicinity. This is rather crude, made by hand just as the Guanches did, without using a potter's wheel. He insisted we should take home a small jug and basin as a memento of our visit. Fortunately we had some cigarettes with us which we gave him in return, for it is not always easy to repay these hospitable people.

Having gone into some detail about people who live in caves, we next visit a place where they live in an extinct volcano. The Pico de Bandama stands 1840 feet above sea level, and there is a superb view from the top, but it is the almost perfect crater which stirs the imagination. For in this crater, some 1000 feet below the crest of the volcano, are several farms, the lava-enriched soil producing good crops and food for the livestock raised here.

When we were here first the only access to the farms was on mule-back down a rough track, but now a narrow road has been built to enable a jeep to get up and down.

This is truly a case of living in splendid isolation.

Up on the heights near the crater top the Las Palmas golf club has been built, with its club house only a little distance from the mouth of the crater – if we had been playing we would probably have spent more time looking at the view than the ball, but perhaps familiarity breeds contempt even of such a panorama.

From Bandama the return journey to Las Palmas is made through the district known as the Monte, which extends as far as Tafira. Here is the main source of the island's best wine, Vino del Monte, a strong red. But in recent years many of the vineyards have been grubbed out, for wine growers have found they can make more money selling their land to the property developers, who build houses in this pleasant garden district for the wealthy Canarios and retired foreigners, than they can from producing wine.

This has always been a popular summer resort, and there are many gracious old Canario homes set in luxuriant gardens. One garden which is open to the public is the Jardin Canario, where all species of plants, trees and palms found in the islands can be seen growing in a very pleasant setting.

For those with only a very limited time to spare for sightseeing, a short excursion to Santa Brigida and Bandama is the most popular for tourists coming to Las Palmas on cruise ships.

Lastly we will go south to the fastest growing and largest beach resort in the islands, Maspalomas and its satellites, a place for holidaymakers who demand only sun, sea and sand – or perhaps sun and swimming-pools in high-rise hotels built to international standards.

Leaving Las Palmas we take the highway past the city's desalination plant and power station; past factories and great complexes of plastic hot houses where cucumbers and roses, carnations and melons are grown for the export market; past fields of tomatoes held upright on a forest of canes where women in wide-brimmed hats tend the precious crops which form such an important part in the Canario economy.

It is uninteresting country, which, if you arrived by air, you will already have seen on the way in to Las Palmas from the modern airport of Gando. It was at Gando that Juan Rejón and his forces made their first landing in 1478, and the desolation of the country with its petrified lava streams and arid fields probably helped influence his decision, on the advice of the legendary Santa Ana, to go northwards to the place of the palms.

But before reaching the airport we take a diversion to Telde, the ancient Guanche centre from where Doramas organised his attack on the Spaniards at the battle of Guiniguada. Today it is a very Spanish looking town, with many ancient mansions, and is an important agricultural centre.

The fifteenth century church of San Juan Bautista (St John the Baptist), to which modern towers have been added, is built of blocks of lava in different colours, giving the building a somewhat uneven appearance. But one forgets this when looking at the splendid reredos of carved, gilded wood, reputedly made in Flanders in the fifteenth century. It is said that the sugar plantations around Telde supplied Flanders with sugar, which accounts for the many Flemish art treasures sent from that country to Grand Canary in payment.

Above the altar is a life-size figure of Christ nailed to a silver cross, to which many miracles are attributed by the local people. But the story of how this statue, weighing just 14 pounds, came to Telde is more interesting than any legend.

It was made in Mexico in the sixteenth century by native artists, known as 'Tarascos', who specialised in making religious statues in a special way from a material made from the crushed leaves and stalks of maize. This was sculpted into the desired figure, then dried and painted with a preservative which gave a flesh-like appearance, and the features were then painted on. These lightweight figures were especially made to make them easy to carry in religious processions.

The story is that this statue came to Telde through a wine merchant who had exported Canario wines to Mexico, and while on a visit there he had ordered one of them for his parish church.

In the small museum adjoining the church are a number of ecclesiastical treasures, including a painting of the Virgin, whose face is claimed to be that of Mary, Queen of Scots, for whom the Spaniards always had much sympathy. There are also some interesting Guanche relics in this small museum.

Not far from Telde, off the old road (not the highway), is the mountain of the Quatro Portas or Four Doors, the openings of which can be clearly seen from the road, with a track going up to them. These lead to an immense chamber cut out of the rock, the assembly hall of the council of Guanche nobles who administered the laws of the island. There are also grottoes and a platform where it is thought the embalming of the bodies of noble men and women took place, for, as previously stated, the Guanches were expert at embalming their dead.

In latter years these caves were used to stable goats, and as a storehouse for fodder, but now they have been cleared out and declared a National Historical Monument.

Continuing along the old inland road from Telde, the next place of interest is Ingenio, at least we found it so, for Eugenio, our very capable and pleasant driver during our last visit to Grand Canary, had many friends here and he was very happy to introduce us around.

Ingenio was once famous as a centre for the sugar industry, then when that crop failed its people made baskets and set up looms to weave rag rugs and bags. Today the main industry is lace making and embroidery, that delicate drawn-thread work called *calados*, which you will have seen at the Pueblo Canario, and later may see in the old Monteverdi home in La Orotava, on the neighbouring island of Tenerife.

We called on Senora Ana Hernandez Sanchez, who lives in a picturesque rambling old house with several patios where about 20 little girls were working over wooden frames on which were stretched various articles such as table cloths or pillow cases, which they were busily embroidering. These girls, ranging in age from 10 to 16, were all being taught the art of *calados* by Senora Hernandez, probably the most skilled embroiderer on the island.

The proudest moment in Ana's life was when she won first prize for handicrafts in 1968, and journeyed to Madrid to receive her gold medal from General Franco himself. With the cash prize she also won she started her school.

'This is a very poor village,' she told us, 'so I thought this would be the best way of providing work for our women and girls. I teach them how to make the most delicate embroidery, and then they can do it at home – I have fifty families working for me like this. I buy only the best linen from Barcelona, for all too often you see good work on coarse cotton, and then the tourists don't want to buy. Let me show you some of the orders we get from wealthy islanders when their daughters get married, and also from many people in the Peninsula, as well as tourists.'

And she proudly unpacked a great carved chest to show us a magnificent tablecloth measuring seven yards long and four yards wide, with two dozen table napkins to match, the whole almost covered with the finest embroidery. There were bedspreads fit for the four-poster of a queen; a baby's christening robe which will almost certainly be a future family heirloom; delicate pastel blouses and nightgowns, in fact, everything that could be made by the women to attract money to their poor village.

And as we left Ingenio we could see those women sitting with their young daughters in the doorways of their houses all busily working over their needlework frames.

On the outskirts of Ingenio is a picturesque whitewashed house with what appears to be look-out turrets on each corner of the roof, and in the garden an old wheel over a stone-framed well. To this wheel is harnessed a very small donkey, who will walk sedately round and round the well to draw up the water should you be thirsty and require a drink – all part of the service for those who stop at this Museo de Piedras, or stone museum.

Here, arranged with great care and artistry, is a display of many different stones, crystals and quartz, not from the Canaries, but from all over the world. How they got to this rather remote village we could not discover, but they do interest many visitors who travel by this road.

There is also another school for youngsters learning the art of *calados* here, and one room has been made into a showroom for this work, as well as many examples of basketry and weaving, all of which are for sale. A pergola-shaped patio at the rear of the house has been converted into an attractive place for refreshments.

We continue through rugged country up to Aguimes, with its white painted church with round domes looking like an Arab mosque. It is interesting to notice the villages through here with their square houses made of concrete blocks, sometimes with only two rooms. But as the owners can afford it they add on more rooms, and finally paint the house. Even the churches are built in this way in the poorer communities.

This is seemingly poor country, but at intervals you will see wooden structures that remind one of mineheads. These are wells, sometimes going down 200 feet below sea level before striking water, much of it brackish but suitable for irrigating the precious tomato fields.

Glinting in the sunlight you will also see great silver saucers in the mountains – these are reflectors for the satellites which provide the island's international telephone and TV services.

During the tomato harvest, villagers from all over the island come to these coastal regions to pick tomatoes, whole families working from dawn to dusk to pick and pack ready for export, a scene reminiscent of the days when the East-Enders used to come down from London to Kent each year to pick the hops.

We now rejoin the main highway, which extends from Las Palmas to Maspalomas, travelling through many new and uninteresting villages, a long line of barren mountains on one side and the sea on the other, but with a wide strip of tomato fields demonstrating that this barren land can be made to flourish wherever water is available.

Once the oasis of Juan Grande was the only green spot in this desert-like place, until the owner of vast areas of land in this part of the island, the Marquis de Vega Grande, brought water from the hills. The village of Juan Grande, with its little church and stately manor house is the heart of his estate, but little of it can be seen from the road through the masses of trees.

From here the road hugs the coast, with half-finished shells of hotels and apartment houses – which may be finished and occupied by the time you read this – until we reach San Augustin and Playa del Ingles with their high-rise hotels, serried ranks of apartments, garish restaurants and sun-loving tourists.

Here visitors of all nationalities are catered for, and we saw some fine hotels along this beach, especially the 5-star luxury Hotel Tamarindos, which was opened while we were last visiting this area. One of the Horesa chain which has a number of good hotels both here and in other parts of the Canaries, this hotel has made excellent use of the artistic crafts of the island, particularly the carved woodwork for which the islands are famous.

There is an almost continuous line of tourist

accommodation for some miles before reaching Maspalomas
with its magnificent golden beach on the southernmost point
of the island.

We had not visited this area for some years, and were as-
tonished at the extent of the development. We well remember
coming down here for a picnic – there were no restaurants
here then – and scrambling over the high sand dunes to the
beach where the tall column of the lighthouse stood guard
over a few huts. Nearby was a natural lagoon, the Charco,
surrounded by an oasis of tall palms; its waters in those days
were a happy hunting ground for the naturalists and those
interested in bird life. Today it is the nucleus of a pleasant
park.

A little way inland was the Mercury tracking station where
the flights of the American astronauts, John Glenn and Scott
Carpenter were recorded in February and May 1962. Now
this satellite tracking station has been moved up into the hills
– the new hotels brought too much noise to the formerly quiet
beach of Maspalomas.

We had heard on a former visit that a project was planned
to develop this area, but nothing had prepared us for the
development which met our eyes on our last visit. At least
there is consolation in this gigantic building scheme that it
provides employment for the local people and gives a lot of
visitors the opportunity of sharing the sunshine and the clear
waters of the ocean in this part of the world.

There are regular express buses direct from Las Palmas to
Maspalomas, a journey of about one hour.

Continuing on the coastal road there are numbers of small
developments, and a fair-size complex of attractive holiday
villas at Arguineguin, but the place we preferred was Puerto
Rico, once a tiny fishing village but now a pleasant garden
and beach resort. Carefully planned, there are hundreds of
little villas hidden among masses of bougainvillia, hibiscus,
oleanders and poinsettias, with a discreet shopping centre and
several nice-looking restaurants.

An excellent idea to stop the traffic speeding past these
villas is the building of regular humps on the roads which

wind through the residential section.

There is a pleasant beach made from sand brought from the Maspalomas dunes; a yacht marina well stocked with expensive looking craft, and even a romantic three-masted schooner which makes excursions along this part of the coast. A real paradise for fishermen, it is easy to hire boats, and there are also good facilities for skin-diving and under-water spear fishing, as well as water-skiing, here.

This, for us, is much more pleasant than the mass-production of Maspalomas, and it is to be hoped it will not continue to grow as did its sister resort.

The coast road continues on to Puerto de Mogan, another fishing village, and it is possible to drive inland as far as the village of Mogan and then on a twisting and turning mountain road to San Nicolas and from there to Puerto de las Nieves, which we visited on our first excursion. But we remembered the warning we had received about this same road when in Agaete, and thought it much better to return by the highway, even if it isn't very exciting.

6. Lanzarote

When Jean de Bethencourt landed at Lanzarote in 1402 he established what was then the most westerly European settlement in the world; the first step, as it were, towards the great unknown – and the New World. But once having been conquered, Lanzarote slipped more or less into obscurity, for apart from its early days, it has very little of interest in the way of history. It also remained one of the lesser developed islands and was generally neglected; a fate also suffered by its neighbour, Fuerteventura, occupied at the same time.

Lack of history may well be due to the easy way by which it was overrun and its relative remoteness – it being more or less off the beaten track and away from the main islands. As for development, as well as being remote it was mainly infertile and very dry, with little in the way of water resources and very little rainfall. And more importantly, it suffered from a prolonged volcanic disaster in the 1730s which laid waste half the countryside and drove many of the inhabitants away.

However, that is in the process of changing – not the history, for that has gone – but the development. The island has become aware of the great god of tourism, and new luxury hotels are rising in Arrecife, the capital, and at other developing beach resorts, as well as the ubiquitous holiday villas and apartments that it is hoped will attract new residents from abroad.

On our last visit we stayed at the very comfortable San Antonio Hotel on Playa de los Pocillos out of the town and beyond the airport. With its private beach, swimming pool, air-conditioning and garden, not forgetting the tennis courts and popular night club, it was a far cry from the simple residencia which – except for the Government Parador, was the best accommodation on Lanzarote in 1960 on our first visit here.

But an influx of tourists is something which surely had to happen, for Lanzarote is the most unusual and fascinating island of the archipelago, in fact it can be classed as one of the most unusual places in the world, all due to those terrible eruptions of the eighteenth century.

These covered much of the island with molten lava up to 20 feet deep, on mountain sides, hill tops and on plateaux and plains below. And when the lava cooled it was to solidify into the most weird and twisted shapes to give the appearance of a Dante's Inferno. This landscape was frequently described in pre-astronaut days as 'lunar', and some films having the moon as the locale were filmed here.

Before going on with the exploration of the island and describing its many attractions, we will give a brief résumé of that catastrophe which lasted for six years, from 1730 to 1736. Brief it would have to be in any case, for there are few detailed accounts of it. Perhaps there were at the beginning of the disaster, but as the years passed the inhabitants became used to the almost constant eruptions and simply took it as part' of their normal lives.

The first signs of the cataclysm to come appeared on 1 September, 1730, when the earth opened up at Timanfaya and a mountain rose up from the plain. It was soon belching smoke and flames from the bowels of the earth, and after some days a wide river of lava came spilling over the rim of the newly formed crater to flow down the sides of the mountain. This went on relentlessly for some months, swallowing up fields, houses and even engulfing a number of villages, and flowing down to the sea in such quantity that thousands of fish were killed and washed up onto the shore.

Then it grew quiet as the volcano subsided – only to start up again later, pouring out more rivers of lava and spewing clouds of cinders and ash into the air to settle even further afield. And so it went on for month after month and year after year until it seemed to the people of Lanzarote that it would never end.

Many had tried to rebuild their homes, then in despair had moved away from the ever-encroaching lava, and many had emigrated to Grand Canary and other islands to start a new life.

Finally, in 1736, there was another great eruption, then all was quiet again – and remained so.

In all, something like half the island was covered in lava and volcanic ash, some twenty villages were destroyed and many farms were blotted out. The whole of the centre of the island was a scene of desolation – even as it largely is today. Yet in all this holocaust there was little loss of life; after the first shocks the people came to expect them, and such was the nature of the eruptions that people had ample warning of each outbreak and were able to evacuate their homes and even perhaps get away with their livestock.

But such was the resilience of the inhabitants of Lanzarote that they soon set about the task of again trying to wrest a living from their devastated land, and make even more productive that area which the lava had not reached.

Gradually they cultivated new land and even managed to use some of that which had been affected. But much, the *malpais* (bad land), carved into weird shapes of hardened lava, was totally beyond recovery. But not altogether useless, for it was these lava wastes that were eventually to attract the first tourists to the island, and their numbers have been steadily increasing over the past decade.

We first arrived in Lanzarote in 1960, sailing from Las Palmas in the then oldest inter-island steamer in service, aptly named the *Lanzarote*, which had been built before the turn of the century. And she showed it! She was a dreadful old tub, slow, dirty and with a habit of bouncing around like a cork even in a relatively smooth sea; she seemed to have as big a complement of live animals, including some prize fighting cocks, as human passengers. It was then an overnight journey, taking 18 hours to cover 130 miles, although this did include a stop of about three hours at Puerto del Rosario, capital and port of Fuerteventura.

We were very glad to leave the stuffy confines of the steamer to step into the cool early-morning freshness of the quay at Arrecife. Fortunately the old steamers have long since been replaced by comfortable modern ships.

In those days one walked down the gangplank off the steamer straight on to the quay, then walked across the sea front promenade into the main street, which was very handy both for passengers and for the handling of cargo. Today the old harbour is used for the fishing fleet and as a yacht harbour, the passenger quay having been moved some three miles to the east of the town, involving a 20-minute taxi ride into town. A little annoying to visitors, perhaps, but much favoured by the taxi drivers. On our next three visits to Lanzarote we came in at the new quay, and on the last occasion by air – certainly a much quicker method.

We have seen no great changes in Arrecife since our first visit except along the waterfront. Here a number of luxury and first-class hotels have sprung up, and away to the south are new apartment blocks and villas. The shops fronting on to the promenade are either new or the old ones have been spruced up to cater mainly for visitors, with increased prices to match. But behind this facade the town is much the same, with the small shops, dusty streets and broken footpaths. It is peculiar but all over Spain and the Canaries so many of the footpaths seem to be in bad condition – downright dangerous, some of them when walking at night – or is it because we just have bad luck in the streets we choose?

On the road out towards the new harbour are the new housing developments for the local inhabitants, who are now benefiting from the new-found prosperity brought about by tourism. Also the desalination plant and several factories and fish-packing plants.

But these developments were unknown on our first visit, and not even projected. Accommodation then for visitors was the Parador on the sea-front; the Residencia Miramar, also overlooking the sea, and three or four small pensions in the streets further back. We settled for the Miramar, where we had a pleasant room with a private shower, and were very comfortable. But breakfast was the only meal served here, so the others had to be taken out, either at the Parador or at one of the town cafés, several of which were quite good.

We used to frequent one near the town centre, where we could have a good four-course meal with a quarter litre of local wine for the equivalent of five shillings (as it was then).

And it was here that we often met one of the most delightful characters we have ever known, a member of the local Guardia Civil named Manuel Merida. There was nothing fearsome about Manuel. He was short, mustachioed and always impeccable in uniform, his tricorn black and shiny in the sun.

He stopped us on our second night on the island as we were strolling on the promenade after dinner.

'You are the English?' he asked, and we agreed, at the same time wondering just what we might have done to attract the attention of the Guardia.

But we had done nothing wrong. Manuel was a one-man welcoming committee – unofficial, of course – who liked to meet all foreigners who visited Lanzarote, especially the English. He also had another reason; Manuel was learning to speak English via the BBC language broadcasts, together with the written instructions and records, and with the added help of the few English-speaking visitors, whenever he could find them.

So he was pleased to welcome us – we must take coffee with him, and let him practice his English, please.

We were happy to find Manuel's favourite café was the one we had chosen for our meals, and there we went to have coffee and talk English with our new-found friend. His English was somewhat halting, but he tried hard and was determined to master it. He would stop and ask us to explain any word or phrase in our conversation that he did not know or that was unfamiliar to him, and he would look at us enquiringly when he was stumped for a word.

He asked how long we were staying and was delighted when

we told him probably a couple of weeks.

'Ah, then you can join with our English club. There are four of us, we *all* learn to speak English by radio, the BBC, you understand. We meet here every night, or as often as we all can to practice – and we would like to have our English visitors as honour members during your stay here.'

So we became 'honour' members for the duration of our stay, meeting them in the evenings at our café after dinner. They were all very keen, and took their lessons very seriously, so much so that during each session anybody who lapsed into Spanish had to buy the coffee. Which was a trap for us, for we were always looking for an opportunity to practice our Spanish with sympathetic listeners.

We would ask something in Spanish and four voices would say simultaneously, 'Ah-ha, now you buy the coffee.'

It didn't seem exactly fair to us, but that was the rule. In fact, we never seemed to learn from the experience, for buying the coffee seemed to be our prerogative most evenings. But it was worth it, for these Lanzarote friends helped make our stay so much more pleasant, and we were able to learn much about the island from them while they learned some English from us.

When we sailed back to Las Palmas Manuel was on the ship with us (not the *Lanzarote*, fortunately), going to sit for his examination for promotion to Cabo (Corporal), which he duly achieved. We were to see a lot more of him during the ensuing years, and met his wife and his son and daughter; at our last meeting he had risen to the rank of Warrant Officer. Putting his English to good use he had translated a police textbook on radio telegraphy from English into Spanish, which had doubtless assisted in his promotion.

Sadly, since then we have lost touch with him, and although we made a number of inquiries about him on our last visit, no one seemed to know where he was stationed.

Arrecife is not particularly interesting as a town. It was founded some time after the conquest because it had a relatively safe anchorage, and was guarded with a reef – the word *recife* means reef. There is very little to see there beyond the weirdly shaped decorations in lava on the pleasant promenade along the seafront, and the picturesque old bridge which leads to San Gabriel's Castle, the old stone fort built to defend the town against Moorish raiders and other pirates.

While Arrecife was the port for Lanzarote, in former times the official capital was moved to Teguise some miles inland and out of reach of raiders who made calls here in search of slaves.

The very Moorish-looking market has changed somewhat since we first visited it, although it is still colourful. Many of the older women from the farms still wear the same type of clothes as these people have worn for generations, long black skirts, shawls and either wide-brimmed straw hats or linen bonnets. They call their wares in the same way as Spanish market women have done for centuries, and weigh out their produce, whether it be fish, fruit or vegetables on hand-held scales, using a variety of objects, usually stones, as weights. But there is no need to be worried about being cheated here, for these women weigh up the sales with an amazing degree of accuracy.

Fruit and vegetables, with the exception of oranges and bananas which need more water than is available here, are locally grown, and most, especially the melons, grapes and tomatoes are of very good quality.

Among the changes we have noted is the decreasing number of camels and donkeys which used to wait patiently outside the market. Their places are being taken by cars, trucks, noisy motor cycles and scooters, parked where the four-footed carriers were once tethered.

Camels were until only a few years ago an integral part of country life. They were used to draw ploughs, carry produce to market and provisions back home, and as the everyday transport of the farmers and their families. Their use has now greatly diminished in this sphere, but some farmers still use them and the ungainly beasts can still be seen in most districts. And the camel is certainly not outmoded as a form of transport on the island, for today they are a tourist attraction, used to convey sightseers to the Fire Mountain, and a ride on a camel is part of the novelty of this excursion.

9 *(opposite) Man-made geyser on the Fire Mountains.*

While the town of Arrecife may not have much to interest visitors, there is much else on the island to see, from the unusual farming methods which have been developed both because of the shortage of water here and the great lava eruption which covered so much of the land, to the extraordinary Cuevas de los Verdes (Green Caves) and mysterious Lake Golfo. And above all, that dramatic region of the Montanas del Fuego, the Fire Mountains, and the *mal-pais* which surround them.

Let us leave Arrecife and explore the island.

If your stay in Lanzarote is to be brief you can tour it adequately in two days, one day doing the south and the other for the north.

If spending several days here, or an entire holiday, then time will not be so important and you can tour around as you please and then re-visit those places which have most attracted you. There is a good network of buses on the island, and there are organised excursions by coach as well as drive-yourself hire car agencies. But we advise hiring a taxi, the price of which is quoted for the trip and not per person; quotes are reasonable and especially economic if a number (four is usually the limit) share the same taxi.

This is what we have often done and we think it far the best method of touring the island; in this way you are independent and can go where you wish, stop where you like, and with a driver who knows – or should know – the best places to see, which is a great help even if you have little of each other's language. Bargaining over the price was once accepted practice, but it is not now usual; however, it is wise to fix a price before setting out. Incidentally, if it is a whole day's tour you are expected to provide the driver's lunch, and this is not included in his quote for the trip.

The excursion to the south is the more interesting and for this you will need a full day to see it properly. Soon you will be intrigued, as we were, by stone-encircled hollows in the ground, filled with black lava sand. Further inspection shows that grape vines are growing in the hollows, and they are far more luxuriant than would have been thought possible in such

10 *(opposite) Good Friday procession at La Laguna.*

a dry climate, and surprisingly, produce large and luscious grapes. A good example of how the resourceful farmers have turned one of the scourges of the eruptions to their advantage.

The secret is that Lanzarote, although a fairly small island with a warm climate and hot sun, has a very heavy nightly dew. And the cinder ash and lava sand attract and retain the moisture. So holes are dug and the vines are planted in a bed of soil and ash, then the whole topped up with more ash and lava sand and each night this attracts sufficient moisture to not only keep the plant alive but to make it flourish and bear well; the sparse rainfall is, when it comes, a welcome bonus.

The semi-circular walls are built of black lava stones to protect the growing vines from the winds which are fairly strong and blow for much of the time, and would damage or even destroy the young plants, which are trained to grow outwards over the ground rather than upwards. A treatment you will also see extended to some trees, especially figs. The enclosures for these trees are larger and deeper, but are treated in the same way with lava sand, the trees trained to grow outwards. We have seen fig trees here less than five feet tall but up to 40 feet and more across.

Grapes, melons and figs grown in this way make very good eating; we have enjoyed fruit lunches of these, which were very refreshing on a warm day. As for the wine produced in this strange soil – both red and white – it has a flavour all its own, not altogether to our palate, but quite drinkable. However, it is very strong, particularly the red, so if you take a liking to it – be careful.

As previously mentioned, the rural women still wear the age-old costume of long black skirts, big shawls, with head-scarves beneath wide-brimmed straw hats or linen bonnets. The shawls are not to keep warm (for it is rarely cold here), or for adornment. This is a dusty, windy, gritty island, and the shawl is worn to be drawn over the face when necessary to protect the nose and mouth from the elements – essential if you are working in the fields or riding a camel. The country women work hard out in the fields, tending the tomatoes and the vines. The sun shines fiercely here, and these women want protection against its rays – unlike the foreign tourists who burn themselves brown on Canary beaches as a status symbol, something the island women cannot understand.

And the headgear worn by the Lanzarote women and girls is not only for protection against the sun, it also denotes a woman's marital status. Single women and girls wear linen bonnets, while married women wear straw hats – when a girl marries she puts aside her bonnet for a straw hat. The headscarves which are worn tied beneath the head coverings are white for both single and married women and black for widows.

So if a countryman is looking for a wife he can soon see not only which are the single girls, but also how well they work in the fields, an important consideration for a farmer.

After leaving Arrecife you can take a route leading directly to the Fire Mountains by way of San Bartolomé and Tinajo, or alternatively go past the airport and by way of Tias and Yaiza. We will take the latter, the route we followed on our last tour of this area, and from Yaiza we will first go on to the south coast with some interesting diversions to the west, and reserving the best until last, return to the capital via Yaiza and the Fire Mountain.

The first part of the journey is not particularly interesting. One of the chief features are very square white houses, very common in Spain and the other islands, with a definite Moorish style, reminding us that the coast of Morocco is less than 100 miles away in places. Most likely you will see numbers of camels in use here in the fields, and one farmer we saw was riding a donkey leading two very heavily laden and disgruntled camels, probably taking his produce in to the market.

In Yaiza there is a souvenir shop stocking a wide variety of wares designed for the passing visitor, an indication of the growing tourist trade, for such a shop in a small town like this would have been unthinkable only a few years ago.

From here we took the road to the west and a few miles further on came to Lake Golfo, an unusual and rather mysterious lake. About one acre in extent, it lies at the foot of steep lava cliffs with its outer edges about 100 yards from the sea. But despite this distance its waters rise and fall in concert with the tides of the ocean, so it was assumed that it had some subterranean connections with the larger body of water. But investigations revealed no channels connecting the two. It was further observed that the water of the lake was much saltier than that of the sea; so much so, in fact, that the waters of the two could not be the same.

So the mystery remains unresolved – and the lake waters continue to rise and fall in accordance with the ocean tides.

Another strange fact about this lake is that the colour of the water is very different from that of the nearby sea, the water of the lake being a clear yellowish-green that never becomes cloudy. But this, according to the experts, is due to a particular marine growth which grows on the bottom of the lake; a growth which is also responsible for keeping the water so clear.

The setting of the lake is spectacular, for its cliff background consists of many layers of strikingly multi-coloured volcanic rock, eroded in places by wind and waves into a delicate tracery. Set in the cliff base overlooking the lake is a pleasant picnic alcove where we have had lunch on a couple of occasions – hard Spanish rolls, fresh tomatoes and the local cheese, all washed down with Lanzarote wine.

From El Golfo we drove south and soon came by Lake Janubio, beside whose marshy surroundings were large piles of white which glistened in the sun. These are salt pans, a prominent industry on the island, though as a side line for local use, not export; it is a coarse salt primarily used for preserving fish and other commodities, and not refined for household use.

Some five miles beyond Lake Janubio is the Playa Blanca, the White Beach, at the extreme south of the island. This is still a rather poor fishing village, but aptly named, for it has an extensive beach of fine white sand, and good swimming.

Here there is also a typical village fish restaurant, somewhat primitive, but the food was excellent, as we found on our last visit when we had lunch on a sunlit terrace overlooking the sparkling sea from where our fish had been brought in only an hour earlier. There is good fishing here, and boats may be hired for deep-sea fishing, which is first-class sport in this area.

There is not much else for visitors at Playa Blanca at the present time, but there are plans for development which might well come to something in view of its sun, sand and sea.

On a promontory a little to the east of Playa Blanca is a tower, the Torre del Aguila, said to have been built by Jean de Bethencourt, but facts do not substantiate this. However, it was not far from here that he set up his first settlement of Rubicon with its fort and cathedral – the first Mother Church of the Canaries – but no trace of either of these, or of the settlement, remains today.

And now for the Montanas del Fuego, the Fire Mountains, the island's prime tourist attraction, and at one time about the only attraction it had to offer visitors. Again passing through Yaiza we go to the north, into the real lava land, the *mal pais*, where nothing grows, a weird area of grotesque formations in fantastic colours.

Driving along this road you will come to a most unusual 'taxi rank' – camels lined up in two rows attended by their masters as though waiting for fares, which is just what they are doing. As part of the organised coach excursion (and also available to those travelling independently), you leave your car or coach here and go by camel across the lava sand slopes to a *mirador* or look-out, then return to the road by another route, finishing your trip to the summit of the mountain by the more modern and conventional method of motorised transport.

We did not participate in this experience on our last visit; we have ridden on camels before and they are certainly not our favourite form if transport. However friends who did make the trip told us it was quite an adventure. Each camel carried two passengers strapped into seats slung one each side from a framework fitted over the hump. Once mounted they set off up a steep, slippery slope of reddish-brown lava cinders and sand; in places the track is so narrow that the passenger on the outside seat has a feeling of swinging over space. But not to worry! These camels and their masters have a good safety record. And our friends told us, in addition to the exciting ride, the view from the *mirador* at the top was marvellous.

But even if you do not ride a camel to the top, the view from the summit of the mountain as one looks over the vast lavaland stretching on all sides is remarkable. As fascinating as the view may be, it was something else that first brought tourists here. As one walks the ground underfoot does not appear to be so very hot, but at a depth of six to nine inches its temperature has already risen to some 300° F and at a depth of two feet it is about 800° to 900°.

When we first explored this area with a friend from Arrecife in 1960 there was nothing here but a tumble-down shanty whose main stock seemed to be unappetising, dried-up rolls, stale cheese, with local wine and warm Coca Cola. The roads were crushed lava and very rough, and you had to walk part of the way from where the road ended.

Our friend had come prepared to show us some of the strange marvels of this lava-covered country, and his first demonstration was to thrust some brushwood into a hole in the side of the mountain. This started to smoke and smoulder within a few seconds, then burst into flames about a minute later, all caused by the terrific heat in the ground just below the surface.

For his next demonstration he put some water in a large tin and placed it partly in the hole; the water boiled within a couple of minutes and he threw some potatoes into the tin to cook. From his 'basket of tricks' he took some eggs, and these were buried in the lava sand by the hole. Finally another tin of water was boiled, this time for the tea, made with tea bags.

This tea was most welcome and the potatoes were scooped out and eaten with salt, but the eggs were rather sulphurous for our tastes. Certainly, it was a very novel meal, and our friend told us that people had been known to fry bacon and eggs and grill steak and chops here, just using the natural heat of the ground, but we did not have such provisions with us to do this – even if we had wanted to.

But things have changed since then and become much more sophisticated. Now there is a first-class restaurant at the top of the mountain, built mainly of lava blocks, and with wide windows giving a magnificent view of the surrounding *mal pais*. It serves a variety of good food, and we were very interested to visit the kitchens to see food being cooked on stoves using the natural heat piped up from the ground.

Outside there are demonstrations of the phenomena that we had seen performed by our friend on an earlier visit, but these were much more professional and elaborate – no do-it-yourself exhibition here. Now there is a staff to give the demonstrations, testing the heat of the ground, burning the brushwood and so on, as well as a new attraction – the geyser.

At intervals a bucket of water is poured into a hole in the ground, the demonstrator quickly jumps back out of the way, for within seconds a jet of boiling water and steam is shot some 15 to 20 feet into the air – a most impressive performance.

The next stage is a tour of the desolate lavaland, which must be taken in special coaches provided for the purpose. Private cars are not allowed here, as in this wilderness of narrow roads carved through the lava only one-way traffic is permitted and it is necessary that the position of all vehicles on the roads be known. We had made some of this trip on our first visit, but the roads were not nearly so extensive then as now, and much of this part of the tour was new to us.

The road was narrow and winding and every turn revealed breathtaking views of this incredibly tortured landscape with its weird colours and shapes stretching for miles on all sides. Even though we had seen it before, it was fantastic and awe-inspiring in its immensity.

And the impressions created by this awesome landscape were heightened by the taped music and commentary played in the coach throughout the tour. This created an atmosphere that was as weird and dramatic as the scenery through which we were passing; the music had been taken from the background score for the film *Odyssey 2001*. We must admit we found it a little overpowering after a time, but it was a good gimmick and certainly in keeping with the surroundings. Altogether, it makes an impressive and unforgettable tour.

Before we left we took a last look over the country we had just traversed and beyond. Stretching out in front of us in all directions were a vast number of extinct volcanoes, their open mouths gaping skywards – although of course we could not see those; one would have to be in a helicopter or a plane to appreciate that angle. There were, we were told, some 300 of these craters in the area.

And as we gazed over the scene we wondered about those fierce powers not so far beneath our feet, and where else they might lie hidden in this landscape. Would they burst forth again sometime, as had happened in the past? Or could such forces ever be harnessed to be put to beneficial use in this energy-starved age, as they were doing in the kitchen of the restaurant on the mountain? It was a comforting thought, but we wonder if anybody will follow it up.

The Montanas del Fuego may also be reached from the capital by going through San Bartolomé and Tinajo, the camel rank being about half-way between the latter town and Yaiza.

And if time is really short and you have only one day in which to tour the island it is possible to see something of both north and south by omitting Playa Blanca and instead have lunch at the restaurant on top of the mountain. From there the tour can be continued through Tinajo, San Bartolomé and Teguise, then northwards through Haria. The return trip follows the east coast road back to Arrecife. We have done it this way, and it certainly allows you to see almost everything of interest, but is rather tiring.

The northern part of the island is less extensive and the scenery somewhat different. Not as unusual as the south, for here there is much less lavaland, less desolation, a more fertile and greener country; a softer and perhaps more pleasing, but less dramatic landscape, but interesting, none the less.

The attraction of Teguise lies mainly in its history. It was named after a Guanche princess (notice how many of the

Guanche names begin with T), daughter of the last king of the island, and who married Jean de Bethencourt's nephew and successor, Maciot.

For a time it was the capital and administrative centre, these functions being moved from Arrecife, as it was inland and less vulnerable to Moorish raids which were frequent in the first 200 years after the Spanish occupation. The main church, San Miguel, is not outstanding, but inside over the altar is a much venerated statue of the Virgin.

According to tradition this was stolen from its place in the church by a Moor who made off with it, perhaps to hold it to ransom. But he was chased by a large dog who forced him to flee after abandoning the statue, which was then recovered. A small painting at the feet of the statue records this event.

In Teguise is the workshop known as the School of Handiwork, and here you can see a craftsman making timples, a musical instrument something like a small mandolin, which is essentially Canario, and used to accompany their dances. If he is at work spare a few minutes to watch him.

Outside the village, on the top of a steep hill, is perhaps the most imposing of Lanzarote's historic buildings, the Castle of Guanapay, erected to protect the Spanish garrison from Moorish raids, and now called the Castle of Santa Barbara.

Travelling on the road to Haria, the commercial centre of the north, we climb up nearly 2,000 feet to Cuesta de los Valles. From this vantage point we have a fine view into a longish valley made productive by generations of hard work by the peasants. They have terraced the steeply sloping hillsides and with the help of cinders and lava sand have created vineyards and groves of fig trees. Common all over the Canaries, this terracing of hillsides is not so usual in Lanzarote where there are few valleys to adapt to this type of farming. At the end of the valley Haria can be seen in a setting of hundreds of palms, which with the surrounding green countryside, gives the appearance of a veritable oasis.

To the west, towards the coast is the little chapel of Los Nieves (the snows); it is odd but there is an obsession in the Canaries concerning snow in relation to churches and chapels, even here in Lanzarote which has never seen it. And, of course, this chapel has its legends.

The Virgin of this chapel had the reputation of safeguarding the lives of seafarers, and one morning when the priest went into the chapel he found the Virgin's robes dripping with water, clear evidence that she had gone forth during the night to the aid of a ship in distress.

Past Haria, a pleasant enough town but of little interest to visitors, the road ends at La Bateria del Rio, on the extreme north of the island. The first part of its name comes from the fact that there was once a fort here with a battery to defend the strait separating Lanzarote from its satellite island, Graciosa. But where is the river to account for the second part of its name? There is no river here, but the strait, which is a mile wide, was given the name El Rio (the river) by the early Spanish. It was near here that Bethencourt first landed, but did not stay, instead making his way to the south of the island.

And it was in this general area that one of the first films with a lunar setting was made.

The island of Graciosa has an area of about 10 square miles, and has two villages, both mainly concerned with fishing. However, it has some good beaches of golden sand, and naturally these have generated the idea of developing it as a tourist centre. Already some villas have been built to attract visitors, but so far there has not been a great deal of enthusiasm – yet! The islet can be reached by a boat service operated by a resident of Graciosa, but this must be booked beforehand through an agent in Arrecife. There is good fishing all around here.

Heading back to Arrecife by the eastern road, the Volcan del Corona is passed soon afterwards, then a short branch road leads to the Cueves de Los Verdes (the green caves) and the Jameo del Agua, the two principal show places of the northern part of the island. We are not always enthusiastic about caves, but must admit the Cueves de Los Verdes are magnificent examples and well worth the diversion and the time to visit them.

Claimed to to be one of the most extensive systems of

volcanic caves in the world, they have only recently been fully explored, but have been known and used for centuries. The Guanches used them as places of refuge from slave traders and piratical raids from both Moors and Europeans, and in latter years the Spanish settlers used them for the same purpose.

With the coming of more settled times they fell into disuse, but in recent years the tourist officials of the local Cabildo realised their potential and once again they have been put to use, but for a different purpose, and a profitable one. The artistry used to stress their characteristics has been skilfully and tastefully carried out, an area in which so many projects of this kind fail miserably.

The galleries of the caverns extend over some four miles, and about half of these have been opened to the public. Paths have been cut in the volcanic rock and the trip through the caves takes one past extraordinary formations, some as weird as anything seen in the area of the Fire Mountains; at one point the path narrows to skirt a very deep cavern, then goes alongside a quiet and limpid lake. In some sections the paths are rough and rather steep and care is needed.

Then we come to a large cave with a roof stretching some 150 feet above. The lava roof and walls are in a great variety of colours which include nearly all the shades of the spectrum – and all highlighted by clever illuminations.

Finally we arrive at the 'Concert Hall' complete with stage and seating for about 1,000 spectators. The acoustics are perfect, and piped music, softly played, fills the cavern. Concerts are staged here occasionally, but unfortunately, never at a time when we have been here. What a magnificent setting for orchestral performances it must be – rivalling the great cave in Gibraltar.

Nearby, but in a separate area, is the Jameo del Agua, a very lofty volcanic cavern which is now a popular restaurant and night club, to which one descends by a flight of curving, rough-hewn steps. Here a local designer has shown considerable ingenuity in using the natural formations of the rock to turn this into an unusual setting for the purpose, using hidden lighting, exotic plants and soft music very effectively, with a small dance floor cut from trunks of pine trees. Here also is a lake, which according to the time of day is illuminated by shafts of natural light from fissures above, which light up the clear waters with a range of colours according to the angle of the sun's rays. A species of blind white crabs, unique to this lake, inhabit its waters, but we have never actually seen them ourselves.

It is an easy run back to Arrecife on a fairly flat road through country of no spectacular scenery, but much of it covered with lava solidified into weird shapes, looking as if it was still molten and malleable. In the parts which have escaped the lava farmers have ploughed small fields and many are planted with a thorny cactus, prickly pear, which is also used instead of fences to enclose other fields. The sight of these cacti growing here and elsewhere on the archipelago and also in Spain has often reminded us of our native Australia. There the prickly pear is a pest and a scourge, and its cultivation is an offence with severe penalties for even having plants growing accidentally on your land; there they must be eradicated and completely destroyed.

However, at one time it was a very valuable commercial crop in the Canaries, and particularly so in Lanzarote, for it was on the spiny leaves of the prickly pear that the cochineal bug was cultivated. This bug was then crushed to produce the cochineal dye, a very valuable export in the nineteenth century, until the industry was practically killed by the introduction of modern aniline dyes, when the exporting of the natural dye fell to almost nothing. However, there is still some small demand for cochineal dye for special purposes, and some farmers continue to cultivate the bugs, which bring them a modest living.

The fruit of this cactus, which the Canarios call *hicos picos,* although rather forbidding looking with its sharp prickles, is delicious to eat. But one must be careful to peel away the outside skin, and make sure all the spikes are removed as well as their roots, otherwise you will have an extremely sore mouth and lips with considerable irritation, even pain for some days.

On our first visit we were very uncertain about trying these prickly pears, but later we had them as a dessert when we were dining at the elegant old Taora Hotel in Puerto de la Cruz, in Tenerife, and found them delicious. It was fascinating to watch the dexterity with which the waiter peeled the spiky fruit – but he did put on gloves to do it.

Another thing we found interesting, especially for Anne as a cook, are the outside ovens. All over the island we saw ovens and cooking facilities built outside many of the farm houses, the ovens sometimes being of brick, but more usually of stones or lava blocks cemented over. Here the women do their baking, both bread and also meat or fish and vegetables in clay pots, and one day as we passed one house the delicious smells of baking bread caused us to stop and inspect the oven more closely.

The baking was just being completed as we arrived and the woman was in the act of bringing out the loaves with a long-handled wooden scoop. She showed us what she had made and invited us to sample the rough, flat bread, made without any rising ingredients. This we did, and the hot bread, eaten with slabs of fresh white cheese was as nice a snack as ever we have enjoyed, even if a little indigestible.

On our last night we had a simple but pleasant meal in Arrecife, at our favourite restaurant, a meal similar to those we had enjoyed when we were 'honour' members of Manuel's English Club – and we thought back on those days, more than 15 years ago. And wondered where Manuel and the other members were now. The next day when we flew out from the small but modern airport en route for Tenerife it was with the usual feelings of regret – and the oft-made resolve to return once again to this strange and fascinating island of Lanzarote.

7. Fuerteventura

Fuerteventura is the second largest of the islands of the archipelago, but in population it is second lowest. Its area, 788 square miles, is only seven less than that of the largest, Tenerife, but its population of 20,000 tops only that of Hierro, the smallest island of the group whose inhabitants number about 10,000.

It is an island of mountain ridges, but their heights do not compare with the others; the highest peak being the mountain of Orejas de Asno (the Ass's Ears) in the Jandia Peninsula in the south, at 2,770 feet, with a number of other peaks rising to around 2,000 feet.

Volcanic in origin as are all the islands, it is dry and barren, with great areas of sterile lavaland, and large expanses of desert especially in the coastal areas, giving these parts an almost Saharan appearance. After all, it is the nearest of the Canary Islands to the African coast, little more than 50 miles separating them at one point. All of which tends to make it a rather desolate place, lacking in interest as it does in vegetation.

But wait! While such characteristics may have their drawbacks, they also have their advantages. Great sandy stretches, especially if those sands are white or golden, provide what many Europeans are endlessly seeking – good beaches. And Fuerteventura is now awakening from its centuries-old slumber to exploit its sun and golden sands and take its share of the profitable tourist trade.

This island may well be, historically speaking, the oldest of the group, for if the account of the report sent to the Roman Emperor Augustus by King Juba of Mauretania (as related in the chapter on history) is correct, this would probably have been the island which his expedition visited.

What is more, in that event this island could claim to be responsible for the naming of the whole archipelago, for it was the dogs from here that gave the name Canaria, after the Latin word for dog.

Together with Lanzarote, it must have been the first to have been visited by the privateers and slave traders, both European and Moorish, in the fourteenth century, and it surely was, again with its near neighbour Lanzarote, the first to be visited by Bethencourt and his Normans in the opening years of the fifteenth century.

However, Bethencourt did not set about the conquest of Fuerteventura until two years later, in the closing months of 1404, a task rendered more difficult than had at first been anticipated by the elusiveness of the natives and the ill-will of the followers of his former partner, Gadifer, whom in modern parlance he had double-crossed.

In the following year he transferred his headquarters from Lanzarote to Fuerteventura.

Incidentally, the name of the island is said to have been derived from a remark made in French by Bethencourt when he first landed – *'Quelle forte venture'* (what a great adventure), which the Spanish easily converted into Fuerteventura.

Yet for all its beginnings, Feuerteventura has really little history and very little in the way of ancient monuments. In its early years of Spanish rule – that it, of the Lords of Gomera who retained it as part of their feudal domain until they relinquished their rights to the Spanish crown in the eighteenth century – it suffered a number of Moorish raids, some of which did considerable damage. But then it virtually sank into oblivion.

Dry, barren and generally poverty-stricken, with poor rainfall, infertile soil and little water supplies which resulted in many crop failures and the subsequent frequent migration of the inhabitants, especially the young, to Grand Canary, and even to Cuba and Venezuela to escape the poverty and lack of prospects for the future – no wonder it had a slow population growth.

But now improving water supplies because of the building of desalination plants, and the prospects of more employment arising because of the new tourist development programme is not only bringing back many who had left to seek work on the other islands, but is also attracting the young people to new careers in the hotel industry.

Puerto del Rosario, the capital and chief port, was a dusty, fly-blown and unattractive village when we first visited it, and its accommodation for visitors only one very simple hotel. It had once been called Puerto del Cabras, doubtless because it was infested by goats *(cabras);* they still roamed the streets and the surrounding countryside at that time. We were definitely not impressed.

Even in those days the island was noted for its beaches, but little use was made of them. The only attraction for visitors was under-water and deep-sea fishing, both excellent, as they still are.

Today, Puerto del Rosario is brighter, cleaner and much larger, but it is still really only a village. The port has been enlarged, and with better services; there are more hotels, and with a National Parador about one mile from the town. Beyond that is the airport – it was there on our first visit with one inter-island service a day – now there are three.

And all this is largely due to tourism. Puerto del Rosario itself does not attract visitors, nor does the second town and port, Gran Tarajal, some 25 miles to the south. But in the far north and the far south of the island are a number of good beaches, miles of good fine golden sands, around which hotels and apartments are being built, and more planned. But development is being carried out more slowly than has been the practice on the two major islands. The authorities of Fuerteventura have passed regulations to ensure that such developments will not be allowd to get out of hand, and they are keeping a watchful eye on building programmes.

For instance, hotels and apartment blocks, as well as villas and private holiday homes must be built a required distance from the water's edge so that not only the wide beaches are protected but also the extensive sand dunes. And a maximum height has been set for all buildings.

Fuerteventura may have been late coming into the tourist scene but they are determined not to spoil things by trying to catch up.

'Slowly, slowly', one hotelier said to us, 'but in the end we will do as well as anyone else.'

Most of the hotels already built are attractive, in the three- and four-star categories, and more are planned. And if one could classify beaches, surely many of these would be in the five-star class, for not only are the beaches good but the water around the coast is clear and inviting, a clarity that has ensured the popularity of all kinds of water sports here. Deep-sea fishing is also a rewarding sport in the waters between Fuerteventura and the African coast.

Returning to the historical background of the island, it is interesting to note that when Bethencourt arrived he found two warring kingdoms, one large one in the north, comprising most of the island, and the other small one in the south. This latter kingdom occupied the Jandia Peninsula, around which there is now so much tourist development.

Across this peninsula are the remains of a wall, the Jandia Wall, which is recorded as having been there in pre-Conquest days, and which separated the two kingdoms. This is one of the few relics of aboriginal times, although there are still caves where the the Guanches lived or hid themselves in times of danger from pirates, slave traders, Moorish raiders or Norman adventurers:

The oldest town of the island is Betancuria, situated in the hills about 20 miles south west of Puerto del Rosario, and really only a small village with a population of about 1,000. It was founded by Bethencourt and was the first capital of the island; the site away from the coast was chosen, as was the case of Teguise in Lanzarote, because of the danger from raids from the sea.

This, however, did not prevent the Moors from sacking the

town in 1593, and burning down the church. Another church was built on the site and dignified with the title of cathedral. It has some fine murals and a painted ceiling. Nearby is a cave in which it is said the conquerors held mass before the building of the original church. There is also a museum here with exhibits of ancient Guanche crafts, including a large number of pottery items and some primitive tools.

Up towards the north of the island at La Oliva, is the other most grandiose historical building of Fuerteventura, the House of the Colonels. It was built in the eighteenth century in Canary-Andalusian style to house the military governors – the colonels, and it must have been a fine house in their day. But it has now fallen into decay; with peeling paint and shutters hanging unevenly, it has a sad air of neglect. Unless, of course, by the time you read this somebody may have restored it to make a tourist attraction.

All around La Oliva the government have established experimental plantations growing agave for the production of fibres. The agave grows in hot climates and needs little water, and on this island it grows well in the volcanic sand, its serried rows adding a pleasant note of green to the landscape.

This is hardly the country for casual touring, and there are few 'sights' to attract visitors. There are still a number of windmills scattered over the land for pumping water – where there is any – in order to irrigate the farms. Here are grown tomatoes, cereals, maize and alfalfa.

But many of these mills are now falling into decay as they are being replaced by artesian bores and the new and modern desalination plants supplying fresh water. So in time the old windmills will doubtless disappear, except for the few used for grinding *gofio,* although it is hoped some will be kept in working order as historic monuments.

We almost forgot about those dogs – reputed to have been the ferocious guardians of the island. A native breed still exists today, known as *Bardinos,* and said to be the descendants of the original wild dogs. These are found all over the island and in the archipelago generally, but they are not very fierce; indeed, they are rather gentle in their behaviour and rather shy. But appearances can often be deceptive and they are regarded as good watch-dogs, and many are trained for that purpose and can be vicious at times – so be warned. Incidentally, the Canarios say you can always recognise a true *Bardino*, they have four white feet.

8. Tenerife

Tenerife, centrally placed in the archipelago, partly volcanic, mountainous and often craggy and rugged, is the largest of the islands with an area of 795 square miles and a population of nearly 500,000. It is roughly triangular in shape with a high mountain range running down the centre for more than half its length from north-east to south-west, like a great spine. The sides slope steeply to fertile plains and valleys between the mountains and the sea. Towards the southern end of the range is the highest peak in the Canaries – in fact, in all Spain – Teide, always called El Pico (The Peak) by the islanders; it rises to a height of 12,152 feet. The mountains are largely responsible for some of the distinct climatic differences on either side; on the south it is somewhat warmer with less rain and a drier atmosphere than that on the north side which has more rain and is more humid.

Because of the very mountainous nature of the island it has a wide variation of vegetation, ranging from tropical and sub-tropical on the plains and lower slopes of the mountain ridge, through that of the temperate zone, and, as the altitude increases, to almost Alpine, somewhat reminiscent of Switzerland in places; and some heights rise above the vegetation line.

The upper slopes of Teide are often snow-covered in winter, sometimes with considerable falls; snow can cover the summit while holiday makers swim in the sea less than 20 miles away. And even when the winter snow has melted, the white pumice sand covering the topmost peak gives the impression that it is still covered in snow. In the south and west the country is largely dry and barren, due mainly to past volcanic eruptions as well as to Saharan winds.

When travelling into the mountains it is wise to make an early start as mists frequently come down later in the day and form a thick canopy at an altitude of between 3,500 and 5,000 feet. You can travel through a layer of cloud and then suddenly come out into brilliant sunshine as so often happens on the way up to Teide, when the peak can be seen sticking up from what looks like a sea of white cotton wool.

Tenerife, as described in the chapter on history, was the last of the islands to be conquered and its subjugation was accomplished only after much bitter fighting, some reverses, one severe defeat and one complete evacuation of the invader's forces.

When Alonso Fernandez de Lugo led his men ashore at Anaga on a fine April day in 1493 he was at the head of the most powerful force yet assembled by the Spanish in the archipelago. He brought ashore with him a wooden cross which he set up where he landed, and kneeling before it, prayed for victory, and then made camp and established his headquarters. He was later forced to withdraw from the island, but returned in July 1494, and this time there was no withdrawal; his prayers were answered and the venture ended in complete success.

The landing place became the nucleus of the future Santa Cruz, the island's capital. Today it has a population of some 180,000 inhabitants, with the original section, now the 'Old Town', complete with cathedral – but lacking somewhat the atmosphere of the Vegueta of Las Palmas.

Santa Cruz has had its share of history, and its people have been called on to resist a number of attacks by hostile forces, two of the most determined being by British fleets. In 1656 Admiral Sir Robert Blake, with 36 ships, attacked the shipping in the harbour, caused considerable damage and sank some 20 vessels, many of them laden with treasure, before sailing off without, apparently, trying to occupy the town. In 1797 Nelson tried to take the town – and suffered his only defeat; an event Tinfereños – or for that matter, all Canarios – will never forget. It was this event that led to the city being given the title *Muy Noble, Muy Leal, Invicta* – The Noble, Loyal and Unconquered.

Visitors who arrive in Tenerife by air, as so many of them do these days, miss the best approach to the capital; from the deck of a ship the view is most impressive. The city rising from the waterfront and stretching up into the hills above, backed by the starkly wild and rugged Anaga Range, mountains almost primeval in appearance, enough, one would think, to daunt the most intrepid of those early invaders. Two long quays stretch out, one on the ocean side protecting the harbour, the other running parallel with the Avenida de Anaga, where are located most of the shipping offices and many other commercial houses.

When you step off the ship you are almost in the town, for it is only 10 or 15 minutes' walk from the farthest out berths, or two or three minutes by car or taxi, to the main square, the Plaza de España.

As the main square of the city, this is probably the best starting point for your exploration of Santa Cruz. Here in the centre of the hub of roads which go out in every direction is the impressive Civil War memorial, set in a pleasant garden with seats which are sometimes very welcome after a busy day. There is a lift to the top of the monument, from where there is a good view over the harbour and city.

On one side is the stately stone building of the Cabildo Insular de Tenerife (Island Council of Tenerife) housing many of the island's local administrative offices. On the seaward side of this is the Tourist Information Office, where you can obtain information not only about Tenerife, but also about the other three islands of the Province – La Palma, Gomera and Hierro.

On the second floor of the Council building, but entered through a door in the Avenida Bravo Murillo, is the Archaeological Museum, which we will visit later. Across this same street is the General Post Office; and here, too, the town buses have their starting point and terminal.

In the Plaza de España taxis may readily be picked up; here is the main taxi stand as it has been ever since our first visit when it was mainly noted for the antiquity of many of the hire cars, usually large American models dating back to the 1920s. In fact, one American visitor said to us, 'I often used to wonder what happened to all the old retired cars back home. Now I know – they come to Tenerife'. We became very friendly with one cabby who drove an enormous 1926 Buick, and a very comfortable car it was then, and very good over the sometimes rough roads of the interior. But the taxis are much more modern now.

Off the Plaza de España is the Plaza de Candelaria, named in honour of the patron saint of Tenerife; a statue of the Virgin of Candelaria, the work of the Italian sculptor, Canova (1778) dominates this plaza. On both sides are the tourist shops, run mainly by Indians offering much the same wares that are sold in Las Palmas – but although a free port, Santa Cruz suffers from the same tax effects on prices. Nevertheless bargains are still to be had, as there are many items that are comparatively low priced.

At the point where the Plaza de España leads into the Avenida Anaga is the Bar Atlantico, its shady pavement terrace crowded with tables and chairs. A café and bar, it has long been popular both with locals and visitors, and is generally very full both inside and out. From the terrace there is a very good view over the plaza and visiting ships may be seen through the trees. On our earlier visits here it was very much less crowded and we often sat out there at any hour of the day or night, cool by day but balmy by night, sipped drinks and watched the people, the square and the shipping in the harbour.

And all the time the *limpiabotas* (shoe-shine boys) humping their equipment in large wooden boxes slung from the shoulder, plied their trade. And they never failed to approach one, even if shoes were shining brightly. We occasionally submitted to their ministrations, for it was interesting to watch them at work; and after they finished our shoes really did shine – for a while. Today there seem to be few *limpiabotas* about; many people regarded them as something of a nuisance, but we rather miss them – and their happy, carefree chatter.

The Plaza de Candelaria leads into the Calle de Castillo, the busy main shopping street – and here again shopping can be an adventure. Many things may be bought more cheaply than at home – and others can be very expensive.

At the top of the Calle de Castillo is the Plaza Weyler, named after a former Captain-General of Tenerife. Here at one time was the bus station for the services going to all parts of the island; this is now located some 100 yards or so away, in the Calle Ramon y Caual. Their services are more extensive now, but the station is not nearly so well placed, nor, we thought, not as well run as that which operated from the Plaza Weyler. However, buses are, for the most part, fairly fast and economical, the fares still being relatively cheap.

From the Plaza de España it is comparatively easy to reach any part of the city. Diagonally one can go through the central area to The Park; past the Cabildo Insular through the Old Town; and along the Avenida Anaga and the waterfront to San Andres and the Playa Las Terasitas, the city's splendid, but artificial, beach.

Many people are attracted by the very term 'Old Town', but that of Santa Cruz is not particulalry attractive in the same way that the Vegueta in Las Palmas is. However, there are some rather interesting old streets, churches, shops and houses, although many of these latter were being pulled down at our last visit. In this area is the Iglesia de Nuestra Señora de la Concepcion (the Church of Our Lady of the Conception) the parish church of Santa Cruz, generally referred to by the residents as the Cathedral; it is also the Mother Church of the island. The original church on this site was burned down and the present building was constructed in the seventeenth century, a substantial, but not particularly beautiful edifice with a square tower.

It has a fine silver altar and a baroque gilded reredos, both rather dimly gleaming in the gloom of the church, there is also a fine bishop's chair. And here are preserved two relics very dear to the hearts of all Tinfereños: the Cross brought ashore by Alonso de Lugo in 1493, and two flags captured from Nelson during his abortive attempt to take the town in 1797. Very old and fragile now, the flags are kept in two glass cases. And, perhaps, this is the time to relate this event, the only defeat suffered by Nelson in all his brilliant career. It is a story of heroism, courage – and generosity.

Nelson had been ordered to attack Santa Cruz, and take possession of a Spanish treasure ship reported to be there, and to capture and occupy the city if necessary. He arrived on 19 July 1797 with four ships of the line, three frigates and a cutter, mounting a total of 393 guns, and carrying more than 1500 men to form a landing party. The expedition was dogged by bad luck in that, as it approached Santa Cruz, it met with adverse winds and was forced to lie some distance off the city for five days, thus giving the Spanish time to prepare their defences and call up reserves from internal garrisons, mainly from Icod. So, when on the night of 24/25 July Nelson decided to make the attack, the defenders were ready for him.

He personally led a force of nearly 1,000 men, sailors and marines, in several long boats on a frontal attack on the harbour and the fort defending it. They were met with withering cannon and musket fire, most of their boats were sunk and a large proportion of their men killed or wounded, one of them being Nelson himself, whose arm was shattered by a cannon or musket ball. He was hurriedly taken back to one of his ships, HMS *Theseus,* where a surgeon amputated his right arm – while his men, outnumbered and suffering heavy casualties, were forced to surrender.

In the meantime another landing party under Captain Sam Hood had landed at the north end of the town, having missed the quay. They overpowered a defending party and occupied a square, and there awaited the signal from the main party advising that they had captured the fort. That signal never came, and, surrounded by a much larger Spanish force, Hood found his position hopeless. With consummate gall he wrote a hasty despatch addressed to the defending General, Antonio Gutierrez. It read:

Santa Cruz 25 July 1797

That the troops etc belonging to His Britannic Majesty shall embark with all their arms of every kind and take their boats off if sound and be provided with any other as may be wanting in consideration of which it is engaged on their part they shall not molest the town in any manner by the Ships of the British Squadron before it or any of the islands in the Canaries and Prisoners shall be given up on both sides.

Given under my hand and my word of honour

SAM HOOD

Ratified by
TROUBRIDGE, Commander of the British troops.
p.p. Antonio Gutierrez.

A brave and defiant letter – and one which met with a generous response. General Gutierrez agreed.

In fact, the British were allowed to withdraw with all military honours, carrying their arms. And in the meantime all the wounded British sailors and marines – and there were many – were well treated and cared for by the Spaniards, and given all the medical treatment, such as it was in those days, that they needed before being repatriated to their ships and allowed to sail away.

And not only did the defenders accord this treatment to their captives, but gave to each man a loaf of bread and a bottle of wine. And they also sent a bottle of wine to Nelson. Not to be outdone in these courtesies Nelson sent Gutierrez a cask of English beer and a cheese, and a letter dated the day after his operation – the first letter he signed with his left hand. It read:

Theseus off Tenerife
26 July 1797

I cannot quit this island without returning Your Excellency my sincerest thanks for your kind attention to myself and your humanity to those of our wounded who were in your possession and under your care as well as your generosity to all that were landed which I shall not fail to report to my Sovereign and I hope that at some future period I may have the honour of personally assuring Your Excellency how much

I am

   Your Excellency's
     humble servant
      HORATIO NELSON

I beg Your Excellency will honour with your acceptance a cask of English beer and a cheese.

The British squadron stayed at Santa Cruz for several days, and during their stay the British were allowed ashore to purchase such provisions as they required – and to treat their wounded. Nelson eventually up-anchored and sailed off on 29 July.

And the Tinfereños honour a brave adversary, for in the northern end of the town is a street still called Horacio Nelson. We know it well for at one time we had a flat there.

Of course the people of Tenerife do not forget the glory of their finest hour, either, and as well as preserving those captured flags in the Church of the Conception there is also preserved at the other end of the town at an old battery called the Castillo de Paso Alto and now laid out as a garden, a cannon they call El Tigre (The Tiger) which, they claim, is the one that shot off Nelson's arm. How they identify this weapon as the one responsible, one cannot say – but, somehow, even the most patriotic English visitor does not question.

Incidentally, Gutierrez is also commemorated by a street name – a small one leading off the Plaza de España.

The fort which defended the town at the time of Nelson's attack no longer exists. Called the Castillo de San Cristobal, it was situated on the sea front and occupied part of what is now the Plaza de España, and was demolished in the 1920s. Hence the name of the street leading up from the Plaza de Candelaria – the Calle de Castillo.

Something of the pride of the Canarios in their achievement

over Nelson is demonstrated by the poet Estevanez who, during a visit to London went to Trafalgar Square to view Nelson's Column. He was suitably impressed but very patriotic, for he dedicated a quatrain to it.

> *The higher the statue of Nelson*
>   *is placed*
>   *The higher will be*
>   *The renown of my Navidad* (birthplace)

The only other church of interest to visitors in Santa Cruz is San Francisco, facing onto the Calle San Francisco (almost on the corner of Calle Villaba) and which contains a fine altar and some very good woodwork. This is the society church of the city and very popular for important weddings and christenings. The window of our room at the hotel in which we stayed on one visit to Santa Cruz gave us a grandstand view of the main entrance to the church and we saw a number of these splendid and colourful occasions. Unfortunately the hotel was pulled down some years ago to be replaced by a concrete and glass office block. A pity, for it was very comfortable in the old fashioned way even though it had only a second class rating (two-star) in today's classification style and for room with private bath we paid 110 pesetas – about 14 shillings (70p) – at the exchange rates then prevailing.

Behind the church, in the former Convent of San Francisco, facing onto the Plaza de Principe, are housed the Municipal Library, Museum and Art Gallery. Here are many good paintings by various artists, including a number by Spanish masters. In the museum is kept the original of Sam Hood's letter to Gutierrez.

Around the Plaza del Principe and in that general area are a number of good restaurants, and the social club, the Circulo de Amistad. One of the streets off the square, the Calle del Pilar, leads to El Parque. This park is a veritable oasis of greenery and coolness, especially on a hot day; a delightful place to visit, and take a little time off from the strains of sight-seeing. Among its atttractions are a colourful floral clock, a miniature lake, a wide variety of flora, including palms and bamboos as well as many species from cooler zones. There is also a pleasant outdoor bar and restaurant and little secluded spots to rest – and, perhaps, eat a picnic lunch as we have done, and as do many local residents, for Canarios enjoy picnics. Perhaps the most pleasant of these spots is the Square of the Tortoise.

This is a delightful area, well shaded by bamboos and palms with a small fountain in the form of a tortoise in the centre. But what makes it so interesting are its seats, four of them. They are made of stone, the backs covered with painted tiles on which are depicted episodes of Tenerife history.

The first one shows customs and crafts of the Guanches of the Orotava Valley as described by early Spanish settlers; the second the arrival of the Spaniards watched by Guanches on the shore, reminiscent of the pictures we used to see in our history books showing the coming of Julius Caesar and his Romans watched by the Ancient Britons. The third one shows the Battle of Acentejo in which the Guanches suffered a crushing defeat, virtually ending their resistance to the invaders; and the fourth portrays modern trades and aspects of the island – modern in the 1920s, that is, when these ceramics were made.

Along one side of the park – it is always referred to simply as El Parque – runs the Rambla del General Franco, a fine boulevard. Down the centre are shady palms and trees which makes the Rambla a pleasant place to sit, either by day or by night to sip a quiet drink.

Leaving the park by Calle O'Donnell – another of the many English, Scottish and Irish names found in these islands – you come to the Avenida 25 de Julio (remember the day they defeated Nelson?) and the little square of the same name. Around this square are a number of colourful seats covered with ceramic tiles, each advertising a commodity of the 1920s, when they were originally put there. There is a Buick car of this period, matches, Swiss chocolate, butter, car tyres and other products – some of which are still available and others which are not. The tiles have a new look, explained by the fact that they were renewed a few years ago, but the originals were copied in detail irrespective of whether the products could now be obtained or not. This square is very popular with children who show great interest in some of the long forgotten products portrayed, and although the seats are not very comfortable they are usually all occupied.

One of the seat advertisements which particularly drew our attention was for Mantequilla Nuevo Zealandia (New Zealand butter) which even then was well known in the Canaries. Soon afterwards we were reminded of the ceramic ad. by a notice in a grocer's shop which read 'Mantequilla Australiana'. 'Ah,' we said, 'Australian butter. Let us get some.' But it proved to be New Zealand butter, and when we pointed out the discrepancy to the proprietor he said, in a puzzled tone, 'Well, it's all the same isn't it? Australia and New Zealand they are the same.'

And it didn't make any difference to him when we pointed out they are about 3,000 miles apart.

Across the Avenida 25 de Julio, on the corner of the Calle Viera y Clavijo, is the English church, St George's, a typically English construction in pleasant gardens; it was built about the turn of the century.

All through this area are fine residential houses in a variety of architectural styles, but to see the best of the typical Canario balconied houses – and apartments – it is necessary to cross the Rambla and wander the streets near the attractive Mencey Hotel – five-star and the best hotel in Santa Cruz. Incidentally, the hotel swimming pool, set in colourful gardens, is open to the public for a small charge.

Along the Avenida de Anaga, towards the Castillo Paso Alto, where 'The Tiger' is located, is the Club Nautico, which offers temporary membership to visiting foreigners during their stay. The club has a splendid swimming pool, gymnasium, a bar and a restaurant which serves excellent meals at reasonable cost. On your own, of course, it may be a little difficult, especially if you do not speak some Spanish, but we have found the amenities provided most acceptable, and, as we knew many local residents, both English and Canario, we were able to spend enjoyable evenings there.

The club has a good yacht anchorage which may be used by visiting yachtsmen who are temporary members. The adjoining boatyard has proved, over many years, to be a very helpful stopover for those intrepid sailors who sail across the Atlantic or around the Cape of Good Hope in small craft.

People who plan to stay some time in Santa Cruz, or visit it regularly, may find it well worth their while to investigate guest membership of the Club Nautico. This also applies to the Casino (non-gambling) in the Plaza de Candelaria, and the Circulo de Amistad, of which we were never members, but where we were often guests.

About four miles beyond the Club Nautico and just beyond the fishing village of San Andres, is the Playa Las Terasitas, the new beach resort of Santa Cruz. This wide beach of fine white sand is the result of considerable planning and engineering ingenuity.

Unlike Las Palmas, Santa Cruz did not have a good beach, perhaps one of the reasons it had not become a tourist city. In the late 1960s a group of business men decided that such an amenity could – and would – be provided. They chose as the site the broad, gently curving bay of Las Terasitas, where there was already a beach of sorts, of black lava sand and stony – but their idea was of the golden sands of the Sahara, some 200 miles away across the sea.

First a breakwater was built across the bay, parallel with the beach and about 100 yards out to sea, so that the sand would not be carried away by the waves as fast as it was laid down. Then a fleet of small craft, with an average capacity of about 50 tons each, was assembled, and a method of loading and unloading the sand by means of giant suction hoses was devised.

The sand was loaded into the ships by these hoses, carried 200 miles across the ocean to Tenerife, and then deposited on the beach-to-be in similar fashion. Hundreds of trips were made, and more than 200,000 tons of sand dumped on the shore to create an artificial beach nearly one mile long with an average width of 100 yards and big enough to accommodate some 25,000 people in reasonable comfort if need be.

When we saw it at the end of 1974, the beach was already proving very popular and plans were in progress for hotels, restaurants and gardens to be built in the immediate vicinity to make this a first-class beach resort within easy reach of the city.

In the Cabildo Insular building, with its entrance in the Avenida Bravo Murillo, is the Archaeological Museum of Tenerife devoted to Guanche life and culture and containing the best displayed exhibition. Anyone who wishes to learn anything about the culture, customs, arts and crafts of the aboriginal inhabitants should visit this museum, which is not confined to Tenerife but covers all the islands.

The exhibits are arranged in an easy to follow sequence, with wall plans. There is also an excellent detailed guide to the museum in four languages, including English, in which its history and purpose are described, and descriptions of the exhibits given in simple and concise language; very useful as the descriptive notes in the exhibition cases are, naturally, in Spanish. The exhibits are divided into two sections, anthropological and archaeological. The bulk of those in the former section, including more than 500 skulls, is not on view to the general public, but on show is a representative selection, sufficient to tell visitors all they need to know.

Included among the archaeological exhibits are a wide variety of pottery objects – pots, jars, vases, water flagons and other household equipment, ornaments, etc. – some rather crude and rudimentary, others more elaborate and sophisticated; mill-stones and querns, bone needles, types of clothing, implements of stone, wood and animal bones (the Guanches did not know of iron or other metals) as well as illustrations depicting phases of their way of life. The clothing made from soft goat skins and sewn with the finest of stitches is worth a careful look, especially as the only needles used were of bone.

There are some funerary platforms discovered in several burial caves on the island illustrating that, like the ancient Egyptians, the Guanches followed the practice of mummifying

11 *(opposite) Puerto de la Cruz, Tenerife: house with typical carved balcony.*

their dead. Some well preserved specimens can be seen here, although it is evident that the Guanches did not attain the degree of sophistication in this art as did the Egyptians. On the platforms are also exhibits of some funerary offerings of food in pottery vessels which were found in some of the burial caves.

Leaving the city by the north highway one heads for the university city of La Laguna, the airport and across the island to Orotava, Puerto de la Cruz and the north coast, along a fast, and for much of the way, dual carriageway. The climb at the beginning is steep, for La Laguna, seven miles from Santa Cruz, is at an altitude of more than 2,000 feet. The heavily laden buses, or *guaguas,* are under some strain before they reach the crest of the climb, even the newer up-to-date buses of today. The old rattletraps which were in service when we first arrived made heavy weather of it, and many newcomers often made bets as to whether they would make it or not; somehow they always did.

As one drives up the hill and looks back, magnificent panoramic views of Santa Cruz, the harbour and the coastline unfold before the eyes; nearing the top a *mirador* has been built at Vista Bella, giving a beautiful view indeed; and no one with an eye for a splendid panorama should pass here without stopping and taking it in.

To reach La Laguna it is necessary to leave the highway at a roundabout on which stands a statue that is often mistaken for St. Christopher. A striking piece of statuary, it is actually that of a native of La Laguna, Father Anchieta, a Jesuit missionary born here in 1534, and who gained renown for his work in Brazil.

La Laguna, which has a population of more than 50,000, was the original capital of the island and the home of the Conquistador, Alonso de Lugo. Seat of the Bishopric, it is regarded as the cultural centre of the islands. Here was founded the first cultural society and, in 1701, the University of La Laguna, some of whose modern buildings make a striking entrance to the city, and are in marked contrast to the city itself where the old atmosphere has survived, with many

12 (*opposite*) *Sand carpets in the plaza at Orotava.*

buildings dating back to the sixteenth and seventeenth centuries. This resembles a city of old Spain where little seems to have changed in centuries, even despite the motor car and other modern devices, and the quickened pace of life.

Here are to be found the original residences of many of the old Canario families, gracious mansions up to two and three centuries old and with spacious and flower-filled central patios. Some of these patios we have seen at the invitation of their owners, but this is something of a rare treat, for, in the tradition of Spain, the people here do not really welcome strangers into their homes – although this custom is not so marked as it once was.

When strolling around the streets of La Laguna keep an eye out for the old doorways; there are many superb examples of stone-framed, carved wooden portals here, many with ancient heraldic devices above. If any of them should be ajar you may get a glimpse of those delightful patios.

As the seat of the Bishopric La Laguna has a cathedral, a rather massive Romanesque building, and a comparatively recent construction of no great external interest. However, inside there are some very fine candlesticks and altar silver made by a gifted silversmith, Antonio Juan Correa, a native of the city. Also worth seeing is the fine pulpit of Carrara marble and, perhaps most importantly of all, the tomb of Alonso de Lugo, who died in 1525.

The oldest church, La Concepcion, with a curious steeple, also contains some excellent silver work. Other religious buildings are the monasteries of San Augustin and San Francisco and the Seminary of Santo Domingo, formerly a Dominican monastery. In the garden of the latter is an ancient dragon tree, said to have been there before the Conquest and which may be viewed with permission.

A step-ladder leads to a central platform fashioned from its branches and here one can appreciate the old story of how it was possible to hold a mass in the hollow trunk of one such dragon tree, as was said to have been done in Orotava. This legendary tree, recorded as having a height of 75 feet and a girth of 50 feet, was destroyed a little over a century ago.

Two interesting festivals of the city are the procession of Holy Week, and that of Corpus Christi in June. La Laguna is famed in the islands for its impressive and spectacular Good Friday procession which is well worth seeing if you are in Tenerife over Easter.

The Corpus Christi festival features colourful carpets of flowers laid along the major streets and in front of the cathedral. This custom is a feature of this festival in a number of places all over the archipelago. The story of the floral carpets is told in detail on pages 122–6.

We had an amusing experience here, demonstrating that evenings in La Laguna are quite cold with chill winds, even in spring, and and also with the difficulties that can be encountered with a foreign language when one's knowledge of it has been aquired by learning it as it 'should be spoke'. While waiting for a part of the Holy Week procession we turned up our coat collars to shut out the chilly, mist-laden wind, and a man standing beside us commented with a shiver, *'Vien free. Vien free.'* We looked at him, puzzled, and he repeated the expression two or three times before we realized he was saying *'Viento frio'* – 'cold wind'. Many not-so-well educated Canarios have a habit, also to be observed in Andalucia, of completely dropping the last syllable of a word. So *'viento frio'* becomes *'vien fri'* (free). A typical example is *'peseta'* which becomes *'peset'*.

Back on the Highway we soon come to the airport of Los Rodeos, the siting of which has been criticised ever since it was built; it is situated in a pocket in the hills notorious for mist, fog and low cloud which frequently closes its runways. Many a time we have sat in the terminal building waiting for the weather to clear. It is a fine modern international airport now with first-class amenities, so different to those we first knew here. And it is all to be scrapped, for a new international airport is being built in the south, near El Medano – and which may well have come into operation by the time this book is published. Los Rodeos will probably eventually be taken over by the military.

Shortly after leaving the airport the golf course is passed, 18 holes with an excellent clubhouse. It was once regarded almost as an English club, most of the members and players being British; however it is now much more international.

The road here is bordered by thick-trunked eucalyptus trees, and on a hot day the scent of their leaves overpowers even the smell of petrol and diesel oil fumes. There are also a number of attractive and colourful bungalows with lovely gardens on one side of the road along here, while opposite them plastic hothouses produce roses and carnations for the European markets.

Here the highway narrows to a two-lane road, and for some distance there is little chance of overtaking except in light traffic. When it is busy with slow-moving trucks – as is often the case – progress can be frustratingly slow. The main trouble, we were told, is the difficulty in taking over some of the land required for widening this section. However, after a few miles we are back on the dual carriageway again and a fast run either to Orotava or down to Puerto de la Cruz – which is usually known simply as Puerto.

We remember this road as it was formerly, narrow and tortuous with numerous tight bends, and the journey between Santa Cruz and Puerto (25 miles) took anything from an hour to an hour and a half. On each of our successive visits to Tenerife we would find the new highway had progressed a few more miles, with the route alternating between the old and the new roads. Now it is completed except for that stretch near the golf course and the last little bit to Puerto. We would be sorry to see those lovely eucalypts cut down, but traffic hold-ups are frustrating, even in the *mañana* atmosphere of the Canaries.

The new highway bypasses several villages that were once on the main road; these can now be reached by short diversions. But this time we will drive straight on and visit them later by another road.

Eventually the highway sweeps around a bend and continues on, to the left to Orotava, and to the right, on the old road, lies Puerto, tourist Mecca of the island. The view is breathtaking, with acres and acres of green banana plantations, the sun glinting on the water tanks and highlighting the faded red tiles of the farm-house roofs. Giant brilliant scarlet poinsettias line the roads while the sparkling sea makes a background for the high-rise hotels and apartments of the popular resort.

This is not the same view that Humboldt saw, and saluted as the 'finest valley in the world', when observing it from what used to be known as Humboldt's Corner, but which was cut off when the new highway was built. The valley is considered to be the remains of an immense crater enclosed on one side by the cliffs of Tigaiga Range, and the vegetation in Humboldt's day was very different to that which is seen today.

But it is a view we have always admired and we were always pleased to see it again when we returned to our little house set against a banana plantation when this valley was our home.

The road dips down past the Jardin Botanico, opposite which is the new luxury five-star Hotel Botanico, which was opened with much splendour during our last visit, and we spent a very pleasant weekend there before leaving the island. There are a number of hotels and apartment buildings on this road, which goes on into the centre of Puerto and to the sea front.

The growth of Puerto over the past ten years or so has been phenomenal, exceeded in these islands only, perhaps, by that of the Maspalomas complex in Grand Canary. However, Puerto does have an advantage over entirely new resort developments in that it was centred on an old-established town, retaining at least some part of its old dignity. There are those who would doubtless prefer Maspalomas, but Puerto is much more to our liking – and not simply because of past associations.

When we first arrived in Puerto in 1960 there were fewer than half a dozen first-class hotels – three new ones on the waterfront, and up on the slopes overlooking the town, the elegant Taoro, old but very comfortable and offering good food and old-world service. Some older second-class hotels in the town centre were also very good value; modernised, they are still very good value today.

One of the main meeting places of the populace, both native

Canarios and expatriate foreigners, was a pleasant square, Plaza Franco, in which was the Bar Demonico, shaded by enormous laurel trees. Here the nightly *paseo* or promenade of the boys and girls of the town took place, and at festival time the merry-go-round and ferris wheel would add their tinny music to the general noise – without which no festival is complete.

Down by the old port was the fish-market and a tumble-down fish restaurant; both have now given way to new developments, and a modern fish-market has been built elsewhere.

That restaurant we remember well. It was a grubby little place with a most uninviting appearance, but they did serve the most wonderful fish meals and some of the best *mojo*, that hot Canary sauce, we have ever tasted. And it was here that we first ate *papas arrugadas*.

It was also the meeting place of a number of foreign literary and artistic people – writers, painters, poets and so on. These included a Swede, a Dane, a German, a Frenchman and a couple of other nationalities we have forgotten. And they took it in turn to speak each other's languages. Each night one of them would ask in English 'What language tonight?' and the answer would be 'Let us speak French', or 'German' or 'Swedish' or whatever; and sometimes it was English, although there was not a Britisher among them. That point settled they would settle down happily to talk – and each with an adequate knowledge of the language of the night to carry on long and animated conversations. The only surprise came when one of them said, 'Let's speak Spanish tonight.' Apparently they had not previously thought of that.

We wonder where most of them are now. Some we know are still in Puerto, another went to Mallorca, one to the United States and another home, wherever that might be. But they did have fun in those days, spoke a variety of languages fluently, were good at whatever they did – and they never seemed to make any money. But they were a very happy lot.

The paved plaza in the old town centre is still as it was, with its colourful flower beds and tall trees, dominated by the parish church on one side and on the opposite side the attractive building of the local tourist office. The old hotels are still there, and facing them a street of simple single-storey houses; it was in one of these houses that at one time we took lessons in conversational Spanish from a charming lady who wanted to improve her English; an excellent two-way arrangement we fulfilled by talking English and Spanish alternately at each lesson.

In this area are old shops we once knew well and which have changed little over the years, but many others have been replaced by modern boutiques, or small hotel and apartment buildings; we noticed numbers of these latter had swimming pools on their roofs. Turning a few corners we come to a narrow thoroughfare fronting on to a rocky promontory where is the rock-pool which is much frequented by the local children. Here on this traffic-free street one can buy practically anything, from Scandinavian furs to Venetian glass, Spanish shoes to stuffed baby crocodiles, the latter from the Moroccan traders who come here to sell their tawdry wares to the tourists. There are several galleries here exhibiting paintings of local artists – some are splendid while others are hideous, but all seemed expensive.

Rising at the end of this street is the fishermen's ancient chapel of San Telmo, restored but with all its simple character after two centuries at least. It is still used, but not as a fishermen's chapel but as an interdenominational church for visitors. On Sunday mornings we have seen, separately, congregations of French, Germans and Swedes attending services here.

Beyond, we come to the wide sea-front promenade and an area dominated by that new forest of concrete and glass hotels and apartment blocks. A tourist paradise.

But Puerto has one drawback; there is no beach worthy of the name. However, every hotel has its own swimming pool, and most have their own extensive private gardens as well. And there are three large pools open to the public; two large and splendid pools in an attractive and popular complex called San Telmo, which also includes a patio and gardens, and a restaurant and bar. And there is a public rock pool built into the sea. Puerto's only beach is of black sand edging rock-strewn waters; we usually prefer swimming in the sea, but here it is the pools for us.

We, who once lived here, might not like all that has happened in Puerto in the passing years, but we must admit that it is a first-class resort which has just about everything for people's holiday enjoyment – except a good beach, and there are many who couldn't care less about that. And we still think, if one gets a little out of the town, not a bad place to live either.

As with so many resorts there is not a great deal to see in Puerto – the old square in the centre of the town, the Fishermen's Chapel and, on the outskirts, the Jardin Botanico de Orotava (Orotava Botanical Gardens) for Puerto was formerly known as Puerto de la Orotava, once the port for this area of which Orotava is the centre, and was important for shipping out wine, cochineal and bananas.

The gardens were established in 1788 for the express purpose of providing suitable acclimatisation conditions for plants from tropical Central and South America destined for gardens in Madrid and other parts of Spain. There is also an impressive memorial to its founder, the Marquis de Villaneuva.

On the road leading up to Orotava (that is the alternative route to that passing the Jardin Botanico) there is the British Club and Sports Centre, where British expatriates have provided themselves with a breath of home; there has been a British community here for a very long time. The Club accepts temporary membership from visitors. Further on is the British School, built on land donated by the Yeoward family (one of the British firms that was long established here) where there are both English and Spanish pupils, and English teachers. Behind the school is the British Library which, it is claimed, has the largest collection of fiction written in English outside the British Commonwealth – South Africa excepted. The English Church – and very typically English – is nearby.

It was up this way, in the District of La Asomada, backed

by an extensive banana plantation, that we had our little house. A small, two-storeyed white house overhung with pink and red geraniums which we called our 'Casita Blanca'. That, outwardly at least, does not seem to have changed any.

Orotava, or more properly, La Villa Orotava, but, like Puerto, normally shortened to the single word (although generally shown on maps as La Orotava), four miles from Puerto and some 1,000 feet above its former port, is a proud and picturesque town of about 25,000 inhabitants. It is very hilly with some extremely steep and narrow streets in which can be seen a number of fine old mansions. Their great stone doorways, flush with the pavements, are surmounted with ancient coats-of-arms, and these seventeenth- and eighteenth-century patrician houses are well named *'Casas de los Balcones''*, for they have some of the best examples of Canario balconies in the islands.

Orotava lies on the slopes of hills overlooking the sea, and at the entrance to the Orotava Valley, lush green areas of bananas plantations, a valley backed by high mountains crowned by El Pico. A situation which results in frequent mists and occasionally quite chilly weather, and it is usually much cooler here in summer than on the plains below. From several terraces, especially one off the main square, there are fine views over the valley.

Of the main buildings there is the Ayuntamiento, an imposing building overlooking a paved square, and two churches, the baroque Church of the Conception with its fine nave and sculptured capitals and the older Church of San Juan, at the top of the town, famous for its painting of the gentle Virgin of Consolation, attributed to Murillo. Both churches have obviously been well endowed in the past; it must be remembered that in the hey-day of the wine and sugar trades this was a very rich town and home of many noble families. It is still a rich town and many of the descendants of the old families still live here.

One house we know well is now part of a chain of centres known as *Artesania* established by the Spanish government all over Spain, where the best Spanish arts and crafts are displayed for sale to the public. This gracious house in the Calle San Francisco was, when we first knew it, the home of the Monteverdi family, one of the oldest families on the island. Its interior carved wooden balconies surrounding flower- and fern-filled patio, with its tinkling fountain, were as fine as those to be seen on the exterior of the building, and the large rooms were filled with splendid carved furniture, old silver and dim oil paintings of family ancestors.

Today it provides a magnificent background for the lovely handwork of the islands, the *Calados,* or drawn-thread embroidery, which is used for everything from handkerchiefs and aprons to enormous table cloths, and you can watch young girls bending over the wooden frames on which this embroidery is done; for this house is also a training school for girls from the country who are taught this fine work. There are also many other kinds of crafts on show here, from pottery to leatherwork, Toledo gold inlay and Seville ceramics, but for us the most interesting thing was to see these girls working at their embroidery in this old house.

We well remember on another occasion coming to this house to watch other young girls – and their mothers – busily sorting out great baskets of brilliantly coloured flowers brought here for the preparation of the floral carpets for the annual Corpus Christi festival and procession.

The custom, now so popular in some parts of the world, of making and laying floral carpets on the streets as part of special celebrations originated here in Orotava. It was in 1847 that the idea of laying a floral carpet in the street outside her home for the Corpus Christi festival was carried out by one of the ladies of the Monteverdi family. This proved such a success that in the next year many of her friends followed this idea and created their own flower carpets for the procession. Soon not only the wealthy householders were taking part, but most of the citizens of Orotava as well.

In 1962 we were again invited to the Monteverdi home, this time not only to see how the flowers were selected and sorted, but how the carpets were designed and all the background work that went into their making. And this was not just for the immediate area in front of the house but also for a number of other nearby streets on the route from the Church of the Conception, where the procession starts.

Head of the house, Don José Monteverdi (then an old man, who has since died) told us that the whole plan of the making of the carpets we were to see in his home was the same as would be followed in many other parts of the town where they were being made – and this is still the procedure followed today.

The country people collect flowers for two or three days beforehand, and bring them into the central sorting depot in the town. Hundreds and hundreds of baskets and boxes filled with colourful blooms; geraniums, hydrangea, carnations, dahlias, roses, daisies, bougainvillia and any other flowers obtainable, are sorted out into types and colours. The scene in the patio of the Monteverdi home was unforgettable while this was going on, accompanied by the chatter of the girls as their busy fingers separated the petals and tossed them into great piles of gorgeous colour, ready for the designers of the carpets.

In another part of the house Don José with members of his family and other assistants showed us how the patterns were made. These were fashioned in metal and every intricate detail was worked out. On the morning of the day of the procession these were laid out in the streets and teams of men and women, boys and girls, working to the designs built up the carpets with flowers, leaves and chopped pine needles, carefully removing the patterns as the work progressed. The results were fine floral pictures, mainly of a religious nature and often representing Bible scenes.

Throughout the day men armed with stirrup pumps patrolled the streets gently spraying the carpets with water, even as their artists and designers were working on them, for June in Orotava can be very hot, and the plants used for the carpets must be kept alive and fresh looking at all costs. By early evening all is finished and what a spectacle the streets and squares of Orotava present – for in all there must be a mile or more of flower carpets, and few cities can show as colourful a scene as this towards sun-down on Corpus Christi – and crowds of spectators line the streets making an appreciative audience.

In another part of the town, in the tiled square fronting the Ayuntamiento, a different band of skilled designers and artists have been making another type of carpet this time using mainly multi-coloured sands instead of flowers.

Covering the entire square, about 15,000 square feet in area, these sand carpets (called *alfombras des arenas*) – there are usually three, each with a religious motif – look like huge paintings, especially when viewed from above, such as from the top of the Ayuntamiento steps or from a balcony of one of the houses overlooking the square. And we found people very generous in allowing us – complete strangers – to come into their houses on these occasions in order to get a good view of the proceedings from balconies and even roofs, and to take photographs.

Created in fine detail of colour and subject, it is difficult to realize that these carpets are not real paintings.

Yet they are made entirely of coloured sands, crushed rock, both green and charred cypress clippings, grasses, chopped corn cobs and gum nuts from eucalyptus treees. The colours cover a wide variety of the spectrum, black, grey, white, yellow, green, red, pink, terracotta, brown and a few shades in between. All materials are collected on the island, the sand and rock coming from Las Cañadas.

The task of creating these carpets involves weeks of careful planning, hard work and the skilful blending of the materials to produce the finished delicate masterpieces – and, above all, extreme patience. The actual laying of the carpets takes several days, and it is enthralling to visit the square and watch the 'artists' at work. as we have done on several occasions.

First the subjects are selected, then the designs cut out from huge sheets of heavy-gauge paper, and these patterns then traced out in chalk on the surface of the square. Then comes the delicate and intricate task of filling in each section of the pattern with the appropriate colours, the artists, and there are generally a dozen or more, working from drawings. And just as the painter works with his palette and brushes, so do these artists work with small boxes filled with the various ingredients required, and a brush; the sands, crushed rock and other materials are carefully laid by hand, but the finishing touches are executed with delicate sweeps of the brush.

The men – and we have only seen men and a few boys – work with an intense sense of dedication. Like all artists one must have a flair for this, and it takes time to learn all the secrets of making a sand picture such as those seen here; hence the boys you may see at work are apprentices, as it were. One of the boys we saw had only one arm – but he worked with grim determination, and was as skilful, if not as fast as the other boys.

We remember on one occasion a few years ago the Ideal Homes Exhibition in London featured a sand carpet and its creators, who were brought over specially from Orotava for the purpose. Some of those who came were old friends we had watched working on their home ground – or rather, perhaps, plaza.

After all this painstaking work by literally hundreds of people, the flower carpets and the sand carpets are complete. Then as dusk descends the procession of church dignitaries, military and civil officials and important guests led by surplice-clad small boys swinging censors and members of the Church Brotherhood bearing flaming torches, come out from the Church of the Conception, with half a dozen men bearing aloft the richly decorated monstrance.

They slowly make their way up through the Calle San Francisco, past the Monteverdi house and then on through the other decorated streets of the town, scuffling through the blossoms as they pass. Finally they reach the plaza, and as the procession crosses the square to the steps of the Ayuntamiento the patient work of weeks is wiped out in a few minutes, leaving only untidy mounds of sand, soon to be swept away by men wielding huge brooms.

But no one minds; that is how it has always been, and, doubtless will always be. The artists in flowers and sand are already thinking of next year's designs. Now small children have their fun and enjoy a battle of flowers, while the more sensitive turn over the blossoms selecting the best to take home – doubtless to weave their own special dreams of the time when they, too, can help make the carpets.

Corpus Christi processions are held all over the Canary Islands in every city and main town, as well as in a number of the villages. And the floral carpets are a feature of many, the most elaborate of which are those of Orotava, La Laguna and Las Palmas (already described in the chapter on Grand Canary). If you are on either island at the time of Corpus Christi you should not miss these processions; in fact, it is a whole day's outing, for it is fascinating to stroll around watching them being made and laid – and witnessing the enthusiasm with which their creators work.

And later in the same month (June) in Orotava is held the colourful Romeria of San Isidro, the patron saint of farmers. On this day all the farmers and their workers, with their families, come into the town, all wearing their traditional costumes – and those of Tenerife are very picturesque. They come in trucks and farm wagons, tractors and even ox-carts, and perhaps a camel or two will also be there, and all decorated with fruit and flowers, palm leaves and corn stalks, representing all the produce of the valley and surrounding districts. They form a procession which winds through the streets of the town, and interspersed among these are groups of musicians and dancers, playing folk music and performing the traditional dances. One of these closely resembles our country maypole dance – although the costumes and setting are very different.

It is a brilliant scene, and everybody joins in, even the littlest Canarios, as they arrive at the Ayuntamiento where the mayor stands to welcome them and wish them good luck for their future harvest.

But that is not the end of the day, of course, for it is then that the real jollities begin. The bars are full and the street stalls do a roaring trade dispensing various local hot delicacies, and groups burst into song and dance all through the town.

And so it goes on until well into the night – or early morning, for, as with the Spanish peoples everywhere, time does not matter when they are out to enjoy themselves on fiesta nights. The last Romeria we attended at Orotava saw us coming home in the early hours of the morning – tired but very happy after a day and night we had thoroughly enjoyed.

Romerias are held all over the archipelago, but, like the Corpus Christi procession, few, if any, equal that of Orotava. However, almost any of them are worth seeing, even those in small villages. The tourist information office or the hall porter at any big hotel can advise where the best are being held.

There are many excursions available throughout the island, but easily the most popular is that to Las Cañadas and Teide, and should not be missed. There are several routes which can be taken by private car or taxi, but the one usually taken by tour coaches is by way of Orotava, then a steady climb up the north side of the central mountain range, turning and twisting through forests of chestnuts against a background of Canary pines. Our last trip was in November, when the chestnut trees gleamed gold in the sun, and small children stood beside the road with plastic bags of glossy conkers they had collected – and hoped we would buy. It was amusing to see these little Canario children playing conkers just as English children do at home.

As we continued up every turn of the road provided magnificent views; in the distance the green slopes of the banana plantations contrasted with the rocky coastline and the blue-green sea. By the sea, prominent for many miles, the towering hotels and apartments of Puerto, and stretching from the coast the Tagaiga range of mountains. And always fresh views of El Pico.

The vegetation changed too, ranging from sub-tropical to almost Alpine as we climbed higher, with great forests of pines planted by the government forestry department. And scattered through the pines are plenty of picnic tables and benches for the benefit of those who like to eat outdoors in this spectacular scenery.

There are some odd rock formations, too; keep an eye out for one appropriately called the Dahlia. It is on a slight rise above the road and looks like a giant dahlia cut into the rock; if you are in a tour coach or a taxi you will not miss it for the driver will stop and point it out. This is described as an unusual work of nature, but, frankly, we have our doubts. It looks too perfect not to have been cut by man – or, at least, man must have given a few finishing touches to nature.

The summit of the road, more than 6,000 feet above sea level, is reached as it sweeps around an almost right-angled bend, and there in front is the beginning of Las Cañadas, a wide, deep crater stretching into the distance; surely one of the world's most spectacular volcanic craters. Some experts say that in prehistory Teide rose from this great crater, which at a later date then sank well below the base of the mountain. Whatever did happen this is an awe-inspiring sight today.

A short drive and then we arrive at El Portillo (the Gateway) where the road from Santa Cruz and La Laguna, which runs along the central mountain range, joins the road from Orotava. Here you will find a number of holiday homes, as well as a restaurant and a bar.

Continuing on this road one sees a world of chaos solidified in rock; what appears to be rivers of molten clay have been hardened immovably by time into smooth waves, while different coloured lava spread out centuries ago by volcanic eruptions has taken on weird and fantastic shapes. At times the wind wails like a thousand Guanche spirits, almost blowing you off your feet if you venture outside the shelter of your car.

At this height the air is so rarified the light has an intensity that can be the joy – or the despair – of photographers who will find shape and colour here like few other places.

From April until June the shrub *retama*, which resembles our broom, bursts into bloom in this inhospitable region, filling the air with perfume. It attracts vast numbers of bees, and it is claimed that the honey of Teide is something very special. As we come near to the Parador de las Cañadas we

13 *(opposite) Terraces at Vila Flor waiting for the potatoes to come up.*

can see another distinctive and colourful plant, known as the Pride of Tenerife, which grows in an elongated pyramid of rose-red flowers to a height of some six to seven feet as if reaching up to El Pico.

Built in the Canario style and opened in 1960, the Parador de las Cañadas is a first-class place to stay; it has 21 rooms, spacious lounges and a swimming pool, and serves excellent meals. We had lunch here on the day it opened; it was very good value then and still is, although the prices have changed somewhat. Anyone who is making a leisurely tour and does not have to be back at an hotel the same night might well consider booking in here for the night. For in addition to the comfort of the Parador, the air is fresh and invigorating (remember it is some 6,000 feet above sea level) and, after the crowds and tour coaches have departed, all is very quiet and peaceful.

It is pleasant to sit outside in the evening sipping a pre-dinner drink and enjoying the magnificent view of Teide; but not such a good idea for after-dinner coffee as, except in the middle of summer it can become distinctly chilly as the night wears on. As it can be in the early morning too, but once the sun gets higher it quickly warms up; it can be cardigan weather around 7 or 8 o'clock but by 9 o'clock can be just right for a pair of shorts and a light shirt. We knew one couple who came up for the night – but did not return to Santa Cruz until five days later.

And now it is time to have a closer look at Teide, which here looms over all, towering majestically more than 6,000 feet above the Parador. The Guanches venerated the volcano as the home of the gods, and many legends grew up around the mountain.

One legend concerns the great rock mass which protrudes from the crater at the top, giving the impression of being a peak within a peak. This story tells of how the peak of another great mountain on the island of La Palma was blown off during an eruption, hurled across the 80 miles or so separating the two – and lodged neatly in Teide's mouth. But, as with all such legends, scientists came up with logic to spoil the tale.

14 *(opposite) Ancient dragon tree at Icod de los Vinos.*

The rock, they say, was thrown up by Teide itself during an eruption, and being too large to be thrown out, was wedged, immovable, in the crater mouth.

There must have been many volcanic eruptions on the island in the distant past but there have been few in recent centuries, and none from Teide itself (Columbus recorded one in 1492). The most notable since then were at Siete Fuentas, in 1604; Fasnia, in the south, in the following year; Llano des Infantes, 1705; Garachico, 1706, when the then important port of Garachico was destroyed, Chahorra, the Pico Viejo, or Old Peak, 1795; and the most recent, Chinyero, in the south of the island, in 1909.

The ascent of Teide is not considered difficult by experts, and climbers frequently undertake it. It is usual to allow two days for the expedition, reaching the Refugio at Alta Vista, at just under 10,600 feet, in the early evening of the first day; the view then is said to be very good. The final stage of the ascent is started early the following morning so as to arrive at the summit by sunrise, said to be an unforgettable experience. On a clear day there is a magnificent view over the island, and beyond, stretching to all the other islands. The descent is during this second day, reaching the foot of the mountain by evening.

We have used the term, 'it is said', in the above description; not being mountaineers we have not ourselves climbed El Pico. Instead we went up the easy way, for in 1971 a cableway was built from the approach road at the base to the summit, and we were whisked up to the top in something like 15 minutes. Certainly the view from the top was breathtaking, but how far it might extend we cannot tell from our own experience, for on that morning it was far from being the clearest of days.

Normally those who wish to reach the summit in the true climber's way engage a mule and a guide/muleteer, and should obtain permission to stay at the refuge; this refuge was given to the community by an Englishman, G. Graham Tiler. Of course, in view of possible more recent developments, regulations concerning the climb, and its planning, may change, so it is best to enquire at the Tourist Office as to what steps should be taken.

As one leaves the Parador, immediately ahead is a short road leading to a *mirador*, or look-out. From here there is a magnificent view over the crater spread out below, almost like the bed (but a very rough bed) of a vast dried-up lake. To the right are Les Roques (The Rocks), large rock formations carved by wind and rain into unusual shapes. Facing the Parador is a tiny chapel, built, we were told, for those who wish to pray before making the ascent of Teide. We have never seen it open, but our informant said it was plain inside, but very attractive.

From the Parador the road continues on to Boca de Tauce, through high banks of multi-coloured rock lava, some black like coal, others clay-coloured, or the green of copper ore, others yellow as golden sand. It is from this area that much of the rock is obtained which is crushed to make the sand carpets in Orotava for Corpus Christi.

After passing through the Boca de Tauce the road forks, that to the left going down to Vilaflor and Granadilla. We took the road to the right in a north-westerly direction in order to return to Puerto by the northern section of the highway. We continued to skirt the crater for some miles, surrounded by landscape that was still rough and rugged. After leaving the crater the scenery becomes a little quieter and eventually we joined the highway at Chio.

We left the highway shortly afterwards and took a winding road towards the coast to Los Gigantes (the Giants), high steep rocky cliffs descending abruptly into the sea; they may be glimpsed from vantage points on the coast, but can only be seen properly from the water. In a bay near the cliffs a new tourist complex has been developed, with an attractive four-star hotel with a very good swimming pool (the beach is virtually non-existent) and a number of villas and apartments, all conforming to the traditional Canario style; a development carried out with some taste. On our visit most of the hotel guests seemed to be British.

Back on the highway again we next passed Santiago del

Teide, a little white village with a strange mosque-like church. It has four domes – and a steeple.

Some miles further on the highway swings north-eastwards and comes in sight of the north coast, and soon we came to a small lay-by where we pulled in. From this vantage point we could overlook far below a town built in semi-circular pattern to conform with the contours of the promontory on which it was built, and some distance off shore, a great rock. This is the town of Garachico, and its rock of the same name.

Garachico was an important town and a sugar and wine port, said to have rivalled Santa Cruz in eminence until 1705, when it was engulfed and virtually destroyed by a violent eruption. The town was rebuilt, but its importance had gone, for the lava filled the harbour and rendered it useless. Some pre-eruption buildings remain, principal of which is the fort, the Castillo San Miguel, which guarded the harbour and town; it has five ancient coats-of-arms carved over the main doorway. Other buildings include the Church of Santa Anna, the Convent of Santo Domingo and the now disused Convent of San Francisco.

A few miles further along the highway is the turn-off for Icod de los Vinos, generally known as Icod, noted for its dragon tree, and the showpiece of this species in Tenerife. Icod was once an important wine growing centre, but suffered in the same eruption which destroyed Garachico; not that the town itself was destroyed or severely damaged, but the vineyards suffered extensively and the prosperous industry never fully recovered.

However, Icod did retain some measure of importance, and was, at one time a garrison town; it was from here that some of the reinforcements were sent to assist in the defence of Santa Cruz against its attempted capture by Nelson. This demonstrates how long the attack was delayed by the adverse weather conditions in that the Icod troops were able to cover the distance over the rough mountain roads and tracks of those days to arrive in time to help beat off the invaders.

Today Icod is a pleasant old town of narrow, winding and very hilly streets in which there are a number of ancient houses with the traditional wooden balconies. In the centre of the town is a raised plaza, at one end of which is the parish church, and below the plaza the famed dragon tree, the one which is always indicated when a Tinfereño talks of 'El Drago'.

'El Drago' is reputed to be 3,000 years old, a claim which may be very doubtful, but it was certainly old at the time of the conquest. Its great age may be judged from the fact that it has been necessary to give it 'crutches' and even to reinforce its decaying trunk with concrete to ensure its survival. There are bigger dragon trees, but this is the most venerated, and all visitors to this part of the island are taken to see it.

Three miles below Icod is San Marcos, where there is safe swimming from an excellent beach if you don't mind black volcanic sand. A fishing village, it has become a resort with a hotel and blocks of apartments, and amenities such as dressing cubicles and showers, bar and restaurant. However, it is a resort for the islanders, many of whom spend weekends and holidays here. It is still a fishing village, and has a tiny and interesting old fishermen's chapel.

Shortly after passing Icod there is a choice of roads, the lower going through the villages of San Juan de la Rambla and Realejo Bajo to Puerto, and the upper via La Guancha and Realejo Alto to Orotava. The villages are quite attractive but of no special distinguishing features – but the two Realejos are of some historical importance. For it was here that the Guanche resistance finally crumbled and came to an end with their capitulation to the invaders.

These twin villages mark, more or less, the encampments of the Spanish forces under de Lugo, who occupied the commanding upper site (Alto) and the Guanches the lower (Bajo). The remaining Guanches had assembled to make what they knew would be their last stand – but, in reality, it never came to pass. The Gaunche chiefs knew that their people, worn out with years of fighting and that mysterious malady, the *madorra*, were no match for the Spaniards with their great superiority in arms and entrenched in such a commanding position.

They sued for peace and accepted the terms laid down by de Lugo on 29 September 1496, recognising the authority of Ferdinand and Isabella, the Catholic Kings, and being baptised into the Christian faith. The conquest of the Canary Islands was finally completed, 94 years after Bethencourt's landing in Lanzarote.

It was at Realejo Bajo that we witnessed our first match in the oldest traditional sport of the islands, *Lucha Canaria*, (Canary Island wrestling). How long it has been practised cannot be said for certain but there is little doubt that it was a sport of the Guanches before the arrival of the Europeans, and may well date back to the times of the first Guanche inhabitants. For, if they came from the Berber stock of North Africa as is now generally accepted, they may have brought it with them as it is said to resembles descriptions of a similar sport of the Egyptians.

We do not know about that, but we do know it is closely akin to the Borey wrestling of The Gambia, the small West African state; it also bears some resemblance of the Sumo wrestling of Japan. The basic rules of *Luchia Canaria* are simple and comparatively uncomplicated, and the contests are a combination of skill, dexterity, balance and strength – but in which any sort of injury is rare indeed.

There are normally ten men to a team with bouts between one member of each team at a time, and are contested in a ring. That is, a clearing in the middle of the local football ground, the spectators sitting around in a rough circle on the ground, for these matches are, generally speaking, very informal affairs. The teams come out barefoot, wearing very wide, thick canvas shorts, the legs of which are rolled up, and deep-necked shirts.

The object is to force any part of the opponent's body to the ground, and the simple act of an elbow or buttock of one contestant touching the ground constitutes a fall and a point to his opponent. There is no attempt to throw each other, hit or even apply holds such as are used in conventional wrestling. The shorts play an important part, for each contestant grips the legs of his opponent's shorts and attempts to lift him off the ground and then force him down. The grip may change to the shirt, but usually both men concentrate on the nether garments.

Another important target is the feet, for while the lifting strategy is being employed, each contestant tries to get a foot behind one of those of his opponent and trip him up. This footwork is something to watch as one tries the tripping technique and the other struggles to prevent it – and carry out the same strategy himself. And the strain of it all is very evident on their faces.

Each bout generally lasts about a minute or so, but according to the strength of the contestants, they may go on for several minutes. One bout we saw at Realejo went on for nearly five minutes, and we were told of some that had lasted for seven or eight minutes – and of one mammoth tussle that lasted more than ten.

Age is no bar, but we were told that the youngest contestants were usually about 17 and the oldest around the mid-thirties. Weight varies greatly, too, and the men can be thin, light and wiry to real heavy weights – and strong men. Of course the contestants in each bout are usually very well matched – one of the tasks of the referee is to see to that.

In the match we saw at Realejo there were 10 bouts all cleanly fought but strenuously contested, and the crowd was very vociferous – but orderly and very well behaved. Comment was profuse and spontaneous, and there was no lack of advice, or criticism, for the contestants. And the contestants had their say too, for they would frequently walk over to the spectators and harangue them and answer criticism, all accompanied with a wealth of eloquent gestures.

The Realejo team were the victors on this day, and there was much jubilation among their supporters, and, as with all such contests, much arguments about the merits and demerits of the teams and their performances and of the referee, of course – and of what might have been if . . . . But all very good humoured as it had been throughout the match.

Lucha Canaria is, primarily, a provincial sport and mainly takes place in villages throughout the archipelago. However, there are some matches arranged in Santa Cruz (usually in the bull ring), and in Las Palmas, as well as some of the larger towns. We do not compare the relative merits of matches contested in cities or in villages, but we think it is more fun to witness such as those we saw in Realejo, performed in an impromptu ring and in an informal atmosphere. Normally the Tourist Office or hotel porters can advise as to when and where matches can be seen.

Incidentally, we may mention here other routes to and from Teide. There is that along the central mountain range which many people think as spectacular as the road from Orotava. Often referred to as the Carratera Dorsal (or Backbone Road) it is much straighter and for part of its course runs along the crest of the ridge at altitudes from 5,000 to 7,000 feet, and providing some magnificent views.

The turn-off from the main highway is just near the statue of Padre Anchieta at La Laguna, and very quickly the road starts climbing, and after four miles we pass through the village of La Esperanza and are soon in the Esperanza Forest and after another mile come to Las Raices (the Roots), with its sweet-smelling Canary pines, a popular picnic area with Tinfereños. Historic, too, for here, some 40 years ago, was held a meeting that was to change the course of Spanish history, and, to some extent, have its effects in parts of Europe.

On 17 June 1936, in a glen in Las Raices, General Franco, then Captain-General of the Canaries, and his officers discussed their plans for rebellion; a month later Santa Cruz was peacefully taken over, the General flew to Morocco, and then went on to Spain; the long and bitter struggle of the Civil War had begun. A column marks the meeting spot.

Some three miles beyond Las Raices is the Pico de Flores, where there is a mirador from which there are some marvellous views; and even better ones await us as we climb above the 5,000-feet level.

As the vegetation thins and we run along the crest the sides of the range slope away sharply and there are clear views to the south and north. To the south Guimar, its valley and the coast line, and, when visibility is good, to Grand Canary and

Cruz de Tejeda, from where we had seen Teide's peak as though floating on a sea of cloud. To the north can be seen the Orotava Valley, the Tigaiga Range, the north coast line, and possibly as far as Gomera and even La Palma; although not so often for here we are above the cloud level on days when it is overcast in the north.

And we continue to climb until we reach the 7,000 feet level and there is little vegetation, as described previously. Then we descend slightly and come to El Portillo, and join the Orotava road up which we came on our last trip.

Another way is to take the road which branches off to the south after passing the Boca de Tauce (remember we took the road heading for the north last time). This route takes us down to Vilaflor, a delightful little town, which, with an altitude of 4,800 feet, is the highest in the archipelago. The road continues to wind down through a drier countryside – but still quite productive.

This is principally potato-growing country, and the farms are spectacularly terraced on the hillsides. As in Lanzarote, lava sand is spread over the ground to attract dew and moisture from the air, and judging from the results it is every bit as successful. But here it is pumice sand which is used, the terraces having a uniform grey colour before the green of the crops breaks the surface.

When we first passed through here it was not uncommon to see camels at work, but they are something of a rarity now, having given way to tractors. However, oxen, and even cows, will occasionally be seen as working animals.

This road terminates at Granadilla, the 'capital' of the district, an important town and centre of a rich orange-growing district. From here the old main road from Santa Cruz to the south passes through the fertile valley of San Lorenzo to Los Cristianos. There is also a road from Granadilla which goes through San Isidro to join the new main highway which encircles the island.

But instead of starting our trip in the middle, as it were, we will make the complete excursion to the south from Santa Cruz.

The southern highway out of Santa Cruz passes through the industrial area, by refineries and cigarette factories. About ten miles further on a road leads to the new resort of Las Caletillas, where there are some good hotels but no beach. A few miles further on we come to Candelaria, where the image of the Virgin of Candelaria, patron saint of the island, is kept in an impressive basilica, built on the foundations of a much earlier church, Her story dates back to pre-Conquest days, when she was venerated by the pagan aborigines, and later to be also venerated by the Conquerors and taken into their faith.

The story tells of two Guanche shepherds who saw what appeared to be a woman holding a baby, standing beside a rock by the sea. When they spoke to her she did not respond, and when she ignored several more calls one of them picked up a stone to throw at her. But as he was about to cast it, his arm became paralysed and he was not able to move it. Terrified, the shepherds fled and reported the incident to their king.

The king and his people flocked down to the shore and found the statue of the woman still standing where the shepherds had discovered it. They carried it off to their cave village, installed it in a sanctuary and paid homage to it, and, according to their legends, the statue performed many wonders.

Years later, in 1464, a young nobleman of Fuerteventura, Sancho de Herrara, heard the story and went to Candelaria to investigate. He was sure that this statue must be a representation of the Virgin, yet Tenerife was still a pagan land for this was long before the conquest of the island. Deciding that the statue should be held in Christian territory, he requested that the Guanche king should give it to him to take to Fuerteventura, but the request was refused. So, one night, he stole it and carried it off to his island, where it was installed in the church.

But the next morning when the priest entered the church he found the image was facing the wall; he turned it back again. But next morning he found the same thing had happened – so he turned it around to face the right way, a procedure which continued for several days. Then an epidemic broke out which was thought to be a punishment for stealing the statue, and Herrara was forced to return it to Candelaria.

After the conquest of Tenerife, the Spanish again took possession of the statue and a sanctuary was built to house what the conquerors claimed to be a statue of the Virgin. And because of the legend, and as the victory over the Guanches was partly ascribed to her, she became the patroness of the island.

But those who visit the new basilica, completed in 1961, do not see the original statue of legendary fame – nor have visitors to Candelaria for the past century and a half, for this is only a replica. In 1826 the original statue disappeared as dramatically as it had arrived; a freak storm created a tidal wave which swept into her sanctuary and carried her out to sea; she was never recovered. A new statue was made and sculptured after the Mediterranean style of the fourteenth century, and this is the one we see today, still venerated by the people.

The Virgin of Candelaria's day is celebrated on 14 August when thousands of people flock to the village from all parts of the island to do her homage.

The new basilica is not to everyone's taste. However, it is an impressive building standing at the end of a spacious plaza beside the sea. Inside it is light and airy, and with some excellent mosaic work. The dark Virgin, high above the altar, is sumptuously clothed.

Along the seafront wall of the plaza stand 10 larger-than-life statues representing Gaunche kings of Tenerife, supposedly those at the time of the finding of the statue by the shore. Behind the basilica is the old Dominican Convent inside which is the lava sanctuary which formerly housed the statue.

Except for some old Canario-style houses there is nothing else outstanding in the town.

From Candelaria we can take the fast highway near the coast or the old main road further inland. This road is rather narrow and winding but does pass through the old towns on the south coastal strip; however, most of these can be reached by diversions from the highway.

Arafo is the first village, two miles off the old road; a pretty little place on the hillside, it is mainly noted for an ancient pine and a number of dragon trees. Güimar is the first town of importance, the largest of the south. A pleasant place, it is the centre of a fertile valley, has some good buildings and an excellent three-star hotel. It is a town that did not live up to early tourist expectations, for many people, including numbers of foreign visitors, came here for their holidays at the turn of the century, but as time passed they stopped coming. However, many well-to-do Tinfereños have established holiday homes at El Puertito, a little port that once served Güimar, and it is hoped that one day its tourist appeal may revive.

A couple of miles beyond Güimar, off the old road, is the Mirador de Don Martin, from which there is a good view up and down the coast and almost as far as Santa Cruz, which, however is hidden from view; and to the north there is a view over the Valle de Güimar, and volcanic Montana de Güimar.

The route now passes through dry and barren-looking country, much of it covered with small whitish stones, pumice. However, despite its somewhat forbidding appearance, orange groves flourish here, as well as other crops, including tomatoes. This is largely due to the complex system of irrigation channels bringing down the water from the galleries in the hills and distributing it widely through the farms and orchards. Many of the caves seen in this area are said to have been inhabited by Gaunches at one time, and are now used for storage, as they are in some parts of Grand Canary.

The next town of any importance is Granadilla de Abona, but always known simply as Granadilla, which, as mentioned before, is referred to as the capital of this district. It is the centre for the produce of its rich valley – oranges, tomatoes, potatoes and maize. However, it is a town of little interest and we take the road that runs south-east to the coast and El Medano, a new resort with a great potential.

About half way along this road we pass the site for the new

international airport, the preparation for which, on our last visit, was well under way – and if everything goes according to plan could well be in partial operation at least, by the time this book is published. But one never knows in this part of the world. Close to El Medano an important new harbour and dry dock are being planned by a consortium of island businessmen. The Pico de Medano rises like a pyramid at the edge of the sea, a landmark as one approaches the town.

When we first visited El Medano in the early sixties, it was a small fishing village which at best could only be described as unattractive. There was little to be seen; poor looking houses, a rather scruffy little *fonda* and a partly built grandiose looking hotel, the construction of which had been abandoned some time before. Its only claim to fame appeared to be that it had once been an experimental station for balloon flights.

But it did have one excellent feature, a long beach of greyish-coloured sand – although that, too, appeared to be somewhat dirty, in keeping with the rest of its surroundings; but it was subject to a lot of strong winds. Nevertheless, it was one of the best beaches on the island, if not the best, which probably led to the idea of that hotel which had been abandoned. However, El Medano could not be abandoned and forgotten for too long; not with that beach and the ever growing clamour for sun, sand and sea from the inhabitants of the colder climes of northern Europe.

Now the new hotels are springing up, as well as apartment and villas. But the planners say they are determined that the resort will be developed with restraint and taste, and that they will not permit the mushroom growth which has been allowed to mar so many projects in the islands. It is early days yet, of course, but the development to date has been carefully supervised. We visited one hotel right on the beach front and from a balcony there was a view over the extensive beach in both directions, and now clean and well kept; this alone should guarantee El Medano's future prosperity.

'But what about the noise from the jets when the new airport is in operation?' we asked. 'It's only about three miles away.'

All that has been studied, we were told. The positioning of the runways and the direction of the prevailing winds would, fortunately, give maximum protection against aircraft noise, the developers claimed, and they had no fears on that account. Which may well be so, but as we are not experts in that field we cannot pass any opinion.

As to the effect of the wind on the beaches – and we had previously noted how they were swept by winds that blew for much of the time – the developers told us that this aspect had also been studied and the resort was being laid out to give maximum protection against that nuisance too. And as they seem to have planned everything so carefully, that also may well be so, but we could not judge on our last visit as, on that occasion, there was very little wind.

There is still much to be done here yet, and although the village still remains, it could, when we last saw it, do with a little cleaning up and brightening – and improvements made to its few streets. But that doubtless will be attended to – and, all in all, we feel El Medano has a rosy future. A forecast we certainly would not have ventured to make a few short years ago.

It is many years since suggestions were first made to build the airport at El Medano, and it was frequently pointed out that it would be a long way from Santa Cruz, and from Puerto and the resorts of the north. And in the days of the old roads it could well have meant a coach trip of up to four hours to Santa Cruz and five hours or more to Puerto and those other resorts. But with the fast highway of today those times will be cut to half, less than between airports and many resorts in Europe.

And it will be in close proximity to the Costa del Silencio (the Silent Coast) beyond El Medano and the other resorts being developed along the west coast. In fact, in future years it could be an even more central point, touristically speaking, than Rodeos.

Back to the highway for a short run, then we veered towards the coast again through dry and desolate country to see another tourist complex, Ten-Bel, on the Costa del Silencio, started some years ago and now forging ahead, and which we were told we should not miss. 'A new concept in holiday resorts', we were assured.

The odd name is derived from the nationalities of the syndicate which planned the development, Tinfereño and Belgian. It is a large, self-contained entity, with apartments, shopping precincts, with all kinds of shops; restaurants, bars, discotheques, car-hiring agency, swimming pools and various sports amenities. Each section features a different style of architecture, for architects and designers from several different countries were employed, including Spanish, Belgian, German and Italian.

The original area, with two- and three-storey apartment blocks and tree-lined streets of villas is well laid out and has been tastefully developed. Years ago these may have looked more like the newer sections do now; bare, bleak, hot and dusty – for these are further from the sea looking out onto the dry plain, and in this part of Tenerife it can be very hot in summer. In time they may achieve the green coolness of the older parts, but it will take time for the new villas and apartments are much more closely huddled together.

This complex is very popular with Canarios, Spanish from the Peninsula and many other Europeans, but certainly would not be our choice as a holiday venue.

Back on the highway it is only a short run to Los Cristianos, fishing port and now showing signs of becoming a popular resort. It is also the port for the excellent car-ferry service between Tenerife and Gomera. Los Cristianos has long been both a small trading port and a fishing village, but in years gone by its tourists were mainly deep-sea fishing enthusiasts, and fishermen still carry on a lucrative sideline catering for their requirements. It has a small beach enclosed by the harbour. On our first visit we did not think of it as a very prepossessing place, but projects are now in hand that may well attract more visitors. The beach has been cleaned up and the town has taken on a much brighter aspect, with a good hotel and new apartments, and the deep-sea fishing will continue to attract sportsmen.

It will also benefit from the nearby resort at Playa de los

Americas, where there are also new hotels and apartments with more being planned – and it too, will soon, doubtless have its crowds. Incidentally, the name has nothing to do with America.

Back on the highway we continued on through changing scenery – pines and stretches of dry country to the east, and to the west the sea, and, on a clear day Gomera can be seen on the horizon. Some distance along the highway we took a short branch road to the old town of Adeje, a brilliantly white place in a sea of banana-green. It is a typically Canario town in the old tradition, with little in the way of modern architecture – although as we entered it we saw a church in a very modernistic design.

Adeje was the seat of one of the ancient Guanche kings, Tinerfe the Great, who may or may not have given his name to the island as some claim. Surrendered by the Guanches after their final defeat, it became the Tenerife headquarters of the Spanish Lords of Gomera, the capital of whose domain was only 15 miles across the sea. A strong fort was built to keep the Guanches, as well as the negro slaves belonging to the lord of Gomera, in order.

The lower part of the town straggles up a steep street and is not particularly interesting or attractive. But on reaching the main part the streets are wide, tree-lined and shady, very comforting both for local residents and visitors, for this can be a very hot place, especially on a summer afternoon. At the top of the main street is the parish church.

First built in the seventeenth century, it has retained much of its original character. It has a fine carved and painted wooden ceiling which is claimed to date from the original building; also a splendid carved wooden gallery, which was reserved for the noble families. Below were rows of seats for the ordinary people, and behind was an area for the Guanches, many of whom were slaves, who stood or sat on the floor. A cynical resident said to us: 'For six days they were worked, sometimes starved and occasionally beaten, but on Sundays they came here to attend Holy service with their masters, to be taken out again when it was over and shut up in

15 (*opposite*) *Lucha Canaria – Canary Island Wrestling.*

their compounds – or wherever it was they were kept. They must have wondered what it was all about.'

Although the customs of those days can well be imagined when standing in this church, it is a long time since there were such practices here – and it is a very attractive church.

On our visit in 1974 we went up to see the Casa Fuerte, the Fort, and now part of an old farm property, but found that due to old age and the effects of a fire, it had been declared unsafe and was no longer open to the public; and, we were told, nor was it likely to be again. We passed several people walking up the hill who were also looking for it but, like us, had not been told it was closed. There is a good view over the town, especially of the church, from just outside the entrance to Casa Fuerte.

There is not a great deal of interest on this road as far as Chio, where we joined it on our first trip after leaving Teide. Most of the land is planted in terraces down to the coast, mainly tomatoes, potatoes and carnations, made possible by a network of irrigation channels and pipes. However, it is only comparatively recently that comfortable motoring was possible beyond here and the west coast, for the roads were either non-existent, or abominable. But those days are now gone and the highway can be taken to any main destination.

In contrast to the country in this area is that of the other end of the island, beyond La Laguna and the encircling highway. A country of different shades of green with its focal point of attraction the Forest of Las Mercedes, to which we will make our next excursion, the last before leaving Tenerife.

Leaving La Laguna along an avenue lined on both sides with magnificent specimens of eucalypts, we drove into a pleasant valley passing, after about three miles, a road leading off to the left which we shall take later. In the meantime we continue along the valley, with the vegetation changing as we come into the forest, where the trees are largely Canary laurels whose foliage is a rather lighter green than that of the Canary pines which are more prominent in the Forest of Esperanza.

Several miles from La Laguna and some 1,000 feet above it is the Pico del Ingles, where there has been a *mirador* for many

16 *(opposite) Church at Adeje, Tenerife.*

years. From here there is a magnificent view looking down the valley as far as the university city; a delightful vision of pastoral serenity. To the left there are also fine views, but of a different nature – the rugged Anaga massif. And around the *mirador,* the forest. If you come here in the early morning, or the late evening, before the tour coaches have arrived or after they have left, there is a peaceful quiet which pervades everything. In these most pleasant surroundings a time when one can be at peace with the world and quietly commune with nature.

When we were here on our first visits there was a road of sorts leading down in hair raising fashion to the coast near San Andres and Las Terasitas – but we never met anyone who had driven down it. We understand that there is now a better road, but, for some reason, we did not take it on our last visit. but we have been told that it is not too bad, and makes a different run back to Santa Cruz.

Instead we drove back towards La Laguna until we came to the road we mentioned earlier. This goes along the Tegueste Valley, another of the pleasant and fertile valleys of this island. It has two attractive villages, Tegueste and Tejina, where the road joins another; to the left this road eventually joins that to Puerto, but first we turned right for Bajamar and Punta del Hidalgo.

Bajamar was being developed as a tourist resort when we first visited it in 1960, and at least two British tour companies organised packaged tours there. Somehow it has not developed as have so many other resorts, despite the fact that it is within easy reach of the airport and Santa Cruz. Certainly it has a rather confined area with not a great deal of space between the shore line and the steeply rising hill behind. There are now several more hotels and a number of villas and apartment blocks; but although the British still come here, including those on packaged holidays, it has, as often has been the case in Tenerife, become more popular with the Germans.

There is not much of a beach here, but there are two splendid and spacious swimming pools built into the rock of the shoreline with the breakers coming in over the outer walls, so that the water is always moving and with the pleasant freshness of the Atlantic itself.

Two miles beyond Bajamar the road comes to an end at the Punta del Hidalgo, the Promontory of the Gentleman. We were told that the full name was Punta del Hidalgo Pobre, or Poor Gentleman. But no one could tell us who the gentleman may have been, or, consequently, whether he was poor or not.

The run from Bajamar to Puerto, keeping as far as possible to the old road, is a very pleasant one. After passing the Valle de Tegueste we come into the Valle de Guerra, rich and fertile, lush and green, and at the right time of the year full of blossoming fruit trees and bees. Here many of the farmers have continued to grow some of the older crops including sugar cane, which once accounted for much of the archipelago's wealth, and some tobacco, as well as vines, tomatoes, potatoes and, of course, bananas – all growing splendidly in this luxuriant valley.

Thinking of the sugar cane, we wondered if the European shortage of sugar at that time, and the high prices it was fetching would stimulate its growth again in the Canaries. That would certainly be in keeping with former tradition, for in the past the Canarios have tended towards changing crops to suit new demands. But perhaps not now; bananas, tomatoes and potatoes provide a lucrative market – and there is that more recently established, and perhaps still more lucrative industry, tourism, whose future seems to be assured. That is, as far as anything can be assured in these difficult times.

The first town of any size we come to is Tacoronte; an old town, it was once a sugar centre, rich and prosperous; it was also important in the wine trade. The new part of the town is of little interest, but the old part, lower down is well worth a visit. Its major attractions are the seventeenth-century Convent of San Augustin, and the parish Church of Santa Catalina; and a venerable dragon tree by the road. Behind the convent altar is the famous wooden Christ of Tacoronte, said to have been carved in Genoa in the seventeenth century; many miracles have been attributed to it. The Church of

Santa Catalina contains much fine silver work; the rich offerings to the church are said to have come largely from the early sugar and wine merchants of this district.

The dragon tree is not the finest specimen on the island, but it is a very good example.

Below the village, near the sea yet another tourist complex is being developed.

The wine of Tacoronte is held in high regard in the islands; some locals will tell you that it is the best. It is a little pungent for our taste, but on our last visit here we stopped at Las Cuevas Restaurant for a break and refreshment. This restaurant, which has a fine view over the plain below and the sea beyond, specialises in the local wine, and as wide a variety of *tapas* as we have seen anywhere in Spain or the islands to go with it. We settled for goats' milk cheese and a local salami with our wine, and they all went well together.

A little more than a mile beyond Tacoronte is the turn-off to El Sauzal, a charming little village with an unusual church; below the village is another tourist development, Los Angeles. From the cliffs there is a fine view over the headlands to the west.

Another three miles further on, off the other side of the highway, is another pleasant village with anything but a pleasant name; La Matanza de Acentejo – the Slaughter of Acentejo. For this was the site of the battlefield where the Guanches inflicted a decisive defeat on de Lugo's army in 1494.

After de Lugo had weakened the resistance of the Guanches, principally by using their rivalries to his advantage, most of their kings and chiefs submitted to him. But the most powerful, Bencomo, defied the invaders and proclaimed he would resist the Spanish; he was joined by a number of minor princes.

After a few skirmishes, Bencomo lured the Spanish forces into a deep mountain defile where he had entrenched his tribesmen on both sides of the gorge. Then he launched his attack, raining down wooden javelins and stones hurled from slings on the invaders, as well as rolling great boulders down the hillsides on them. The Spaniards, taken completely by surprise were thrown into confusion, suffered terrible casualties, de Lugo himself being wounded, and none escaped. Of a force of about 1,200, some 700 of the Spanish were killed and many of the remainder wounded, and all who survived were taken prisoner. Such records as there are today suggest that the Guanches lost only about 300 killed.

Bencomo could have massacred the entire Spanish force, as some of his supporters demanded, but he spared the survivors and allowed them to retreat to Santa Cruz. De Lugo decided that his position was hopeless and he evacuated his force to Grand Canary.

Three miles further on the next village, La Victoria de Acentejo, recalls the sequel to the above events. Later in 1494 de Lugo and the Spaniards returned,and, apparently, Bencomo tried a similar ruse; but this time de Lugo refused to be drawn by such tactics. He manoeuvred the natives into open battle, and the superiority of the Spanish arms and armament told, for the Guanches were driven back with even greater slaughter, and some 1,500 or so of the Guanches were said to have been killed.

It was the final major battle in the conqest of the archipelago, although there was some resistance for a further two years before the final capitulation at Realejo, which we have already written about.

The Spaniards celebrated their victory by naming the spot La Victoria de Acentejo, the Victory of Acentejo and building a chapel which they dedicated to Our Lady of the Angels — and a church of the same name still stands on that site.

La Victoria is a pleasant little village, often flower-bedecked, and makes a bright display, especially in winter. The same may be said of the next village, Santa Ursula, which also boasts an interesting little church, with an ivory statue of the Virgin.

And shortly after Santa Ursula we are again on the road to Puerto, passing the Jardin Botanico.

9. La Palma

'Ah, you will like it there; it's so green and fresh.'

That is what friends in Tenerife told us back in 1960 when we announced that we were going over to La Palma, the most north-westerly island of the group, to have a look around. And so we found it to be on that, our first visit, and every time we have been there since; it surely justifies the term applied to it here, 'the Green Isle'. This even applies to the east coast, in contrast to Grand Canary and Tenerife; of course, it is much further away from Africa and the Sahara.

La Palma has also, in proportion to its size, the greatest mean altitude of the islands, with several peaks more than 7,000 feet above sea level, the highest being nearly 7,900 feet. It also has the most rainfall, a lot of mist at times, and considerable dew by night. All of which helps to account for that greenery, which includes not only bananas and the other crops normal here, but fruitful orchards and extensive pine forests as well as ferny glades – and waterfalls, of which we have seen but few in the Canaries.

It does have its dry and barren areas but these are not extensive; and it has its lavaland, too, but having nothing to compare with the islands of Lanzarote or Tenerife in extent or spectacular appearance. Which seems a little strange, for it has suffered many eruptions in the distant past and the last of those in the archipelago occurred here, in 1949 and as recently as 1972, although the two of that year were of a comparatively minor nature.

La Palma, or to give it its full name, San Miguel de la

Palma, is shaped rather like a pear – or a heart according to your fancy or interpretation, being broadest in the north and tapering to a point in the south. It is the fifth in size (Gomera and Hierro only being smaller) with an area of 280 square miles and a length of about 30 miles and a width of some 20 miles at its widest part. Despite its size it has easily the largest population after the two main islands, the inhabitants numbering around 80,000. It has the usual crops, and there are extensive almond groves in the north; tobacco also grows well here and there is a tobacco factory. Tourism has made no great impact as yet, but even without this La Palma is considered quite prosperous.

Its history has been generally rather uneventful. Alonso de Lugo landed here in September 1491, and won over the natives by conciliatory methods and by playing, as usual, on their rivalries. Only two tribes resisted; one was overcome rapidly, while the other took refuge in the Caldera de Taburiente, a huge crater and now the showpiece of the island, where they resisted for some months. Eventually de Lugo enticed them out for a parley – and then attacked and slaughtered them. The Guanche resistance was broken and in April 1492 they capitulated – although there were some minor revolts over the next few years. From then on the island had only to contend with sporadic attacks from pirates and privateers; the last serious attack by a would-be invader was an unsuccessful one by Admiral Charles Winton in 1743.

Our first visit to La Palma was also uneventful; we arrived in the late afternoon having come from Gomera in one of the old inter-island mail boats. The capital, and port, Santa Cruz (de la Palma, of course, the other one being de Tenerife) presented a delightful sight, its main area stretching along the waterfront, and straggling up into the green hills. We spent a few pleasant days there and found a friendly, hospitable people only too willing to help foreigners, especially English speaking; few English visited La Palma in those days (and there are not so many now.)

These new friends showed us around and made sure we saw how green was their island. One man even took us to his home, and invited a few friends to make it a convivial evening. This was one of the most pleasant evenings we have enjoyed, drinking wine and eating little tit-bits on a vine-covered terrace overlooking the town. Compact and white, with its neat little harbour, it provided an entrancing sight in the fading light.

Our next visit, two years later, was not so peaceful; in fact, quiet little Santa Cruz de la Palma provided us with the most exciting adventure we have had in our travels around the islands. We had thought to stay at the Parador, but had made no bookings – and we found it full. But we were luckier at the recently built Mayantigo Hotel, so everything was fine. Or was it?

When we registered the clerk took our passports and flipped through the front pages, pursed his lips and gave us a rather funny look. And before we had left the foyer he was already on the telephone speaking rapidly into the mouthpiece, his eyes glued on our open passports. What was that all about, we wondered? In those days Spanish authorities, especially in more remote areas, were sometimes rather inclined to look on foreigners with some suspicion. Could we have done anything to arouse such suspicions? And we were still wondering at dinner time when a big man, whom we were certain was wearing a shoulder holster, sat at the next table in the dining room – and seemed to be very interested in us. We shrugged it off; doubtless our imagination.

But there was no question of imagination when we returned to our room. We had gone straight down to dinner after our arrival at the hotel, leaving our unpacking until after the meal. We opened our bags and at a glance we could see they had been tampered with. We always pack to a definite plan and there was no doubt that our bags had been searched, not with any particular skill, but certainly very thoroughly. That did it. We had to find out what this was all about. But it was getting late and we were very tired so we decided to leave it until the morning.

But it was still not over. Before breakfast next morning we decided to take a picture of the inviting looking swimming pool in which four men were splashing around while another stood near the edge idly watching them. As John raised his camera the chap who had sat at the next table in the dining room the night before suddenly stepped in front of the camera and held up his hand. Almost angrily we demanded to know what this was all about, but he merely pointed to the camera, then to the men in the pool and wagged an admonishing forefinger at us in the manner common among the Spanish for intimating that one should not do something.

It was not until we had made enquiries and complaints officially (later that morning) that we found out what it was that drew this unwelcome attention. Our friend was a policeman – and we gather he did wear a gun; the man who had been standing beside the swimming pool was also a policeman, as was one of the four who had been swimming.

The other three men were members of the O.A.S. who had been active against France's General de Gaulle in Algiers and who had sought asylum in Spain. They had been sent to La Palma, where they were kept under strict surveillance. But what had that to do with us, we asked? Well, our passports did show us as being 'Writers and Journalists' – and foreign journalists were just not the kind of people the police wanted around those Frenchmen.

So that was what it was all about – and we quickly made clear our position; that we were not concerned with news reporting, especially of a political nature, but were purely travel writers – and offered proof. Our police friend was very apologetic – but, naturally, we must understand that he had his duty to do. We did, and so it was all amicably settled. Before we left we had a drink together – when he was off-duty, of course.

On our last visit to La Palma we flew in by a jet prop plane, just over 30 minutes from Tenerife; an airport to take the largest jets was being planned, we were told. The airport had been there on our earlier visits but on our first tours of the Canaries we always travelled by the inter-island steamers; we preferred the more leisurely method – and we did meet interesting people. Coming in by air, however, gives a vivid impression of how green the island really is.

Santa Cruz (which, incidentally was always referred to on our early visits as La Ciudad – the City, or the 'Capital' – and still is by many people) has not changed much in the intervening years. True it has grown, and has encroached a little more up the green slopes as the population has grown, now some 20,000, a few thousand more than when we had first known it. But the town (we beg your pardon, city) is still much the same and its people seemingly as casual and friendly as ever. Tourists would be welcome, we were told, but accommodation has not increased much – if at all; one hotel has gone and another built – but another is planned.

There is not a great deal to see in the capital, but it is a fascinating place through which to wander in leisurely fashion; it can all be seen easily in the course of half a day – but a very pleasant half day. Fronting the sea is a broad promenade, the Avenida Maritima, lined with restaurants, shops and many houses, several with Canario balconies, some double storied; beyond the *barranco* at the northern end is the fishermen's quarter, a colourful little area.

Running parallel with the Avenida Maritima is the main commercial and shopping street, the Calle O'Daly (also known as the Calle Real) named after an Irishmen who came to the island in the early days. It is narrow and rather crowded at all times of the day – except during the siesta – but never breathless or bustling. Here many of the buildings also boast the traditional balconies which gives the street a pleasant old-world air. About half way along from the port end is the palm-shaded, pocket-sized Plaza España, referred to as the 'social centre' of the town – a very small social centre one would think. However, it is a most delightful little plaza, for here are located some of the best architectural features of the Old Town.

Across the street, facing onto this square, is the handsome Ayuntamiento dating from 1563; it replaces a former administrative centre destroyed by marauding French pirates in a raid ten years before – one of the town's livelier historical moments. It is fronted with finely carved pillars decorated with the coats-of-arms of bygone officials, and some excellent murals on the walls flanking the entrance. The inside is modern and the Council Chamber, for which permission to view may be obtained, has a magnificent pinewood ceiling and more murals.

Across the plaza is the parish church of San Salvador, mother church of the island. It makes a most attractive study as seen through the pillars of the Ayuntamiento, and whenever there are groups of tourists in town there is always someone trying to photograph the old church through those pillars; and it takes time, for it is not easy to photograph and the visitors, with their cameras at the ready, dodge all over the place seeking a better viewpoint. The artists are not so bothered; how many of them have painted this enchanting scene over the years?

Although not large, the church, which was built in the early sixteenth century in Spanish Renaissance style, presents an attractive sight, its entrance reached by a wide flight of 11 well-worn stone steps. But it is the classical stone portico, with double columns supporting a fine pediment, rather than the building itself, which dominates the plaza; massive and elaborately carved, it frames the handsome door. Inside the church is rather plain, but the sacristy has a good carved wooden ceiling.

Facing on to the plaza are some late eighteenth-century houses built by wealthy and noble families. A fountain playing in the centre completes this delightful old-world scene.

There are other old family mansions to be seen around the town, some with stone portals bearing the coats-of-arms of their original owners. Among the best are the Sotomayor House and the Palace of the Counts of Salazar, both also in the Calle O'Daly. In this street is another little shaded square in which is the Santo Domingo Monastery, now a school.

At the top end of the Calle O'Daly, is another plaza facing on to the Ravine de las Nieves; on the edge of the ravine is an unusual spectacle – a full-sized replica of Columbus' ship *Santa Maria,* built in stone. On certain festival days it is beflagged, and once every five years is in full splendour, rigged, beflagged and beflowered to celebrate the procession held in honour of Nuestra Señora de las Nieves (Our Lady of the Snows), the patron saint of the island, when her image is brought down from its sanctuary two and a half miles away and paraded through the town.

The sanctuary of Our Lady of the Snows is reached by leaving Santa Cruz by the road on the opposite of the ravine; a rather narrow and winding road which climbs some 650 feet in the two-and-a-half-mile journey. Here, in a tiny square containing a few houses, is the sixteenth-century chapel housing the statue of the Virgin. She stands above an altar of beaten Mexican silver; a figure rather smaller than one would expect for the patroness of the island; nor is she as sumptuously costumed and adorned as one might imagine she would be. Not that this is significant, we were told, for it is said that jewels worth a fortune are lodged in her name in the vaults of a bank in the city.

Her origins are uncertain, but tradition has it that, like the Virgin of Candelaria in Tenerife, she was in existence before the Conquest and was venerated by the aborigines. And, like the Virgin of Candelaria, she was adopted by the conquerors as the island's patroness. Her sanctuary was erected in the sixteenth century. Her day is celebrated on 5 August but it was not until 1680 that the quinquennial procession from her sanctuary to Santa Cruz was inaugurated. Since then she has been carried triumphantly on her own day every fifth year, starting with the first year of each decade, to La Ciudad, passing down the ravine opposite the gaily rigged Santa Maria, through the town and to the church of San Salvador.

Leaving the chapel one can return to Santa Cruz by way of Brena Alta, a delightful little village near to which is a viewing balcony, Risco de la Concepcion, looking directly over the capital with the port in the foreground; it gives a perfect view. A short run through a green and fruitful valley brings us to Brena Baja from where the main road is taken back to Santa Cruz.

The outstanding excursion of the island is that to the

Caldera de Taburiente, claimed locally to be the largest crater in the world. It may well be, for it is enormous and has a depth of 3,500 feet. When we first visited it the only possible approach was by jeep over a devious and appallingly rough road; but that has changed and it is now reached by an excellent road, and a tunnel driven through the mountain. On our last trip we entered the tunnel through a thick swirling mist and came out in brilliant sunshine on the other side, which often happens here; it can be bad weather east of the mountains yet clear on the other side only a couple of miles away. So if the weather is bad in Santa Cruz don't despair – very likely it will be very different on the other side of the mountain.

After passing through the tunnel there is a drive through very green country and after a few miles a side road is taken which runs through more heavily wooded country until we come to the Cumbrecita, where is the viewing platform a short walk below the road. And from it the view is breathtaking.

The crater is, indeed, very extensive and what a different sight it presents from the viewing platform. No great gaping black hole of twisted lava here, no demoniac rock shapes that must have once been apparent, reminders of some Dantesque inferno, of nature in its most horrible and tormented agonies. No, this great crater is covered with greenery from top to bottom; trees up to 40, 60, perhaps even 80 feet and more tall. A smiling crater masking the bubbling hell's cauldron it surely was in some past era.

However, we were told, there are some parts which are still black and bare. And beyond, on the other side of the crater we could see some stark and rugged mountains and the Rocque Los Muchachos (the Boys' Rock), at more than 7,900 feet the highest peak of the island.

We were the only people there at that particular time; it was perfectly still, and the only sound that broke the quiet was the occasional call of a bird in song. A bird who had every reason to sing, for surely this was a paradise. We stayed there for a long time before being brought back to earth by our driver who told us that if we wanted to see the rest of the south we'd better get a move on. We have visited many places in our travels which we have been reluctant to leave and this was one of them. With sighs we went back to the car and settled down for the rest of the trip.

It is possible to go down into the crater, but, somehow, we did not feel like doing so. Those who would like to, however, should make enquiries at the Tourist Office in Santa Cruz before undertaking the expedition.

Continuing on our journey we passed through the charming town of Los Llanos, the second largest on the island, with some attractive houses and a pleasant, shady plaza. From there we swung south to drive through attractive, but in no way outstanding country until we came near the village of Las Manchas, close to which there is a wide black river reaching from a mountain above right down to the sea, a distance of about five miles. Not a flowing river now, but once it had been – a river of molten lava destroying everything in its path. This was the result of the big eruption of 1949 when the Vulcan de San Juan became active on St John's Day, 24 June. The lava flow swept away most of the houses of Las Manchas, destroyed many farmhouses and a large acreage of crops. But no lives were lost, and there were very few casualties. And now, as in most such calamities, the village has been rebuilt.

As we travelled further south we came into lava areas and rather desolate-looking country, although some vineyards were to be seen, and arrived at the village of Fuencaliente, the southernmost village of the island. Fuencaliente is the centre of a prosperous wine-producing area; the wine is light and palatable. Here in the extensive vineyards the vines are trained to grow flat along the ground, as in Tacaronte in Tenerife, so as to get the best advantage from the ground moisture, and we were told, this produces larger and better flavoured grapes.

South of Fuencaliente in a desolate landscape is the Volcan de San Antonio, from which came the eruption in 1677. This volcano was also responsible for the last two eruptions on the island, those of October 1972, minor affairs which caused little damage although adding to the desolation here. And as we walked through the cinders we were reminded of Lanzarote's Fire Mountains, for the ground here was quite warm, as were some small stones we picked up. Is San Antonio just slumbering?

The run up the eastern side of the island is through much well-wooded country, and there are some fine views, but we made only two stops. The first was to make a short diversion shortly before reaching the village of Mazo to visit the Cave of Belmaco, said to be a home of Guanche chiefs (also said to be a council chamber) and in which there are prehistoric rock carvings. We did not find them particularly impressive – and no one has ever been able to tell us with any certainty of their origins or what they might mean.

The second stop was at a *gofio* mill – but this was no old-fashioned mill grinding out *gofio* flour between ancient mill-stones; it was, in fact, completely automated. And its chief purpose was not to produce flour to make the traditional *gofio*, which is still eaten quite a lot on the island, but as a basic mixture for sweets for children.

The north of the island is not all that interesting and it will not worry us if we do not see it again. Once you have visited the Caldera, made the tour to the south and explored Santa Cruz, you have, in our opinion, seen the best of the island – and at least one place like no other in the Canaries. But if you have the time, well certainly take a little excursion to the north.

After leaving Santa Cruz the first few miles of the journey is through rather barren country, but then come the green and fertile areas again. A little distance before Los Sauces is reached, and a mile or so inland from the road, are the Los Tilos Woods, one of the best woodlands on the island, with fern undergrowth and the attractive Los Tilos Waterfall.

Los Sauces is a small town of about 8,000 inhabitants; the centre of a fruitful area it is a pleasant place, but of little interest. We well remember having lunch in a little bar-café there on our first visit, and so unused were the townspeople to seeing foreigners that dozens of school children came along when they heard there were strangers in the town – and we lunched to a large, and, we thought, an appreciative audience. But on our last visit we went unnoticed; that time we had no audience. Even though they still do not have many foreign visitors in Los Sauces.

17 (*opposite*) *Toree de Condé in San Sebastian, Gomera.*

10. La Gomera

La Gomera, roughly circular in shape, is the second smallest of the islands with an area of 149 square miles, and a population of a little over 25,000. It also probably has the most rugged terrain of any of the islands, although its highest point, the mountain of Alto Garajonay, in the centre, reaches only a little more than 4,800 feet abve sea level. The terrain is due to the low mountains which are slashed by numerous deep ravines extending down to the coast.

Although only 15 miles from Tenerife at its nearest point to that island, very little had been done about it touristically until quite recently. This is due, no doubt, to the fact that there was too much interest in developing the two main islands and, more latterly, Lanzarote, and also, despite its proximity to Tenerife, that it was comparatively cut off from the rest of the archipelago, and the world, until after the last war. Up till then there was only the inter-island steamer service connecting it with Tenerife, La Palma and Hierro. And internal communications were very bad, for its only road was the main street of the capital,San Sebastian de la Gomera; and beyond that, nothing. The only communication Gomeros had with their capital and other villages and settlements was by mule track – hard travelling in this rough country. And, of course, they had contact with each other through their unique whistling language.

But things have changed, and are still changing with great rapidity. After the war the frequency of the steamer service was stepped up, roads were built and gradually extended to

18 (*opposite top*) *Replica of the "Santa Maria" at La Palma.*
19 (*opposite bottom*) *Silbadores in Gomera.*

many parts of the island, and these are now in the process of being modernised. And external services have been further improved with the inauguration in 1974 of a car-ferry service between Los Cristianos, in Tenerife, and San Sebastian, with several services daily; and an airport is being planned (it was the only island without this facility on our last visit). A most attractive parador has been opened in San Sebastian, with several hotels being planned as well as holiday complexes and villas in other parts of the island.

One hopes that such development will not spoil Gomera, for it is an interesting and fascinating place, and already an excellent venue for excursions for those staying at one of the more developed islands. However, that is the business of tourism and it will be most welcome to the economy of Gomera, which is lacking in industry – although the new car-ferry service has already given a fillip to the export of agricultural produce. In the meantime we can still enjoy its natural and historic attractions while they still remain uncommercialised and unspoilt – and hoping, of course that they will largely remain so.

Gomera has had an eventful history. It was, for some three centuries, the administrative seat of the Lords (or Counts) of Gomera, whose feudal domain extended over Lanzarote, Fuerteventura and Hierro. In the early days those lords had considerable trouble with their subjects and suffered many raids by pirates and Moorish slave traders, who, on one occasion, practically devastated San Sebastian and killed or carried away something like half the population. And a Dutch fleet made an unsuccessful attack in 1599.

Christopher Columbus was almost a frequent visitor, for he called in at San Sebastian on three of his four voyages of discovery to make his final preparations – his last port of call in the Old World before setting off for the New. And here his name has been romantically linked with the notorious Beatriz de Bobadilla, widow of Ferdinand Peraza the Younger, the former Lord of Gomera.

Beatriz de Bobadilla was quite a woman. She had been maid-of-honour at the court of Ferdinand and Isabella where she had attracted the attentions of Ferdinand. At that time Peraza was in Spain having been sent there to stand trial for his connection with the death of Juan Rejón, who had been killed in Gomera when resisting an attack on his men by the Count's forces.

It was a situation in which Isabella saw a chance to solve two problems at one stroke, thus getting rid of Peraza, who was an embarrassment, and Beatriz, who was a rival. She promised Peraza a pardon and Beatriz a new life if they should marry and depart for Gomera immediately – and stay there. Both readily agreed.

Peraza was a cruel despot whose excesses drove his subjects to a new revolt and in the ensuing fighting he was killed. Beatriz locked herself up with her family in the fortress-like Torre de Condé (Count's Tower) which had been built for defence against pirates – and rebels – and waited for help to come. This arrived eventually, after which Beatriz exacted a terrible revenge on her rebellious subjects.

When Christopher Columbus arrived five years later, in 1492, on the first of his voyages, the fiery widow was at the height of her power, and unattached. To her Columbus went to ask assistance in securing livestock, provisions and water and to make a final overhaul of his ships. Beatriz was ready to give all help, and was also not averse to a little dalliance. They remained close for some weeks, but how far the romance went we shall never know for certain. Columbus was a man of single purpose and did not let anything deter him from the task in hand – and Beatriz did not tell. As soon as his preparations were finalised, he sailed away.

Columbus returned to San Sebastian in the following year on his second voyage, and was enthusiastically received by the widow, but this visit was much briefer. He took on supplies as before and made final preparations, but apart from official visits he seems to have seen little of the Lady of Gomera. When he called on his third voyage, in 1498, Beatriz had married Alonso de Lugo, the Conquistador, and was living in Tenerife at the time, so the two did not meet.

This visit was not without incident, however, for Columbus

found the town was being threatened by French corsairs who made off at the sight of the Spanish ships, abandoning two treasure ships which the Admiral captured. On his fourth and last voyage, in 1502, he carefully avoided the island altogether, making his final preparations in Grand Canary.

And at the beginning of September of each year a 'Columbus week' brings together hundreds of people from many countries who are interested in commemorating the anniversary of the birth of the great explorer – 6 September. Organised by the Instituto de Estudios Colombinos de la Isla de la Gomera (Institute of Columbus Studies of Gomera) the week commences with a fiesta up the mountain of Cedro with folk dancing and plenty of eating and drinking. Throughout the week there are lectures on many subjects relevant to the admiral, from descriptions of his ships and how they were built to a discourse on Beatriz de Bobadilla. Painting and pottery exhibitions are held in the Casa de Colon, dance groups from Spain and recitals of Spanish music entertain members of the Institute and their guests.

Then on the anniversary of Columbus' birth a memorial service is held in the Church of the Ascension in honour of all the brave Spanish navigators who sailed across the Atlantic so many centuries ago. And, appropriately, the week ends with a regatta and the finish of a sailing race from La Palmas to San Sebastian, with the Columbus trophy for the winning crew. Each year representatives of governments from other countries associated with Columbus come to Gomera as special guests for this week, as well as officials from other islands of the Canaries.

This still little-known island of Gomera, takes it connections with Christopher Columbus very seriously indeed.

On our last visit, when we travelled over on the new car-ferry, the *Benchijigua,* we found the capital had grown considerably since we first saw it, and there were some new features, but beneath it all it did not seem to have changed much at all. In the harbour the quay had been enlarged; new houses had been built on the hill overlooking the harbour, and there was the new parador dominating the top of the cliff to the right.

One of the first buildings that visitors will see on landing is the ancient customs house (now a private dwelling) where there is a well from which, according to tradition, Columbus drew supplies of fresh water, as did, so it is said, many other mariners in later years. On leaving the harbour the Torre del Condé is prominent to the left. Built in the fifteenth century, it is structurally much as it was originally, but is now some distance from the sea which once lapped at its foundations.

The main street, which leads out of a plaza adjoining the harbour, is unimpressive, and its two principal attractions are related, as can well be imagined, to Columbus – the house where he is said to have stayed on his first visit, and the church where he prayed and attended Mass.

The house, Casa de Colon, is No. 60. A two-storeyed building, it has obviously been much restored and re-built over the centuries, and was, in fact, undergoing further restoration on our last visit, and was surrounded with scaffolding. It is now a Columbus museum, and a locale for meetings and concerts, especially during Columbus week.

Further along the street, facing the Plaza Calvo Sotelo, is the Church of the Ascension, which some Gomeros refer to as the cathedral. Like the Casa de Colon, it is not very much as it was in Columbus' day; the only part remaining from those days is the south side, the greater part having been built since. It is an unremarkable church, but with some good woodwork, and an interesting mural, unfortunately in poor condition, depicting the repulse of the Dutch fleet in 1599.

But the attractions of Gomera lie outside its capital; rough, rugged country slashed with deep ravines, as well as green and fertile valleys on whose verdant slopes are steeply terraced farms, probably the most spectacular terraces of all the islands; and in the centre, a fine forest. Today much of the island is easily accessible by car, for the main roads are now surfaced, and the majority of those which are not are graded and in fair condition. But there are still a number of roads in the interior which leave a lot to be desired, so, if you bring a car and intend to tour extensively, make enquiries before setting out. A better idea, perhaps, is to hire a taxi, and leave the rest to the driver.

However, if you are content simply to be taken around and shown selected sights on a pre-arranged schedule, there are coach excursions originating in Tenerife which go over on the car-ferry. These tours make it a long day, for they leave Santa Cruz and Puerto very early in the morning and return fairly late at night; but they are very well organised and cover practically all the most interesting places on the island. At the time of writing there were no excursions originating in San Sebastian.

The usual runs are from San Sebastian to Hermigua – the second largest town and sometimes referred to as the 'capital of the interior', and a colourful little place. Then on to Agulo, scene of the picturesque Romeria de San Juan, and to the coast where the road turns westwards and goes on to Valle Hermosa, an enchanting valley with a delightful little town of the same name. From here, by a lesser road, you can go on to Valle Gran Rey (Valley of the Great King) where Gomeros were building themselves holiday villas on our first visit.

Returning to San Sebastian via this road it is a worthwhile diversion to branch off on a side road between Valle Hermosa and Agulo and drive through the Forest of Cedro. This is an area of luxuriant forest growth and has been declared a national park. It is, indeed, an area of great beauty – but it was jealously guarded even before the preservation order. Gomera is a rather dry island and the forest attracts rain, and what moisture there is in the air, and it is therefore invaluable to agriculture. The main road can be rejoined a few miles beyond Hermigua from where it is an easy run back to San Sebastian.

The projected airport is to be built near Playa Santiago, on the south coast; a new road was being built to connect it with San Sebastian when we were last there. There are plans for holiday developments at Playa Santiago.

But what is most striking in Gomera is the ruggedness of the terrain, with deep ravines often running from well inland right down to the coast. Crossing them, even from a point on one side to the other almost directly opposite, perhaps only a few hundred yards across, might well involve an arduous, even hazardous, journey of several miles and some hours. Communications between neighbours could be and often were, very difficult.

Conditions which gave rise to that curious whistling language, the *Silbo* (Spanish for 'whistle'), which is unique to Gomera.

We had heard about it before our first visit; a language where people communicated with each other over considerable distances by whistling. Not, we were informed, by a system of whistled signals, but the language itself, Spanish, in the form of phonetic whistles. We were told that it was introduced in the early days of the settlers who found that such signals used by the Guanches could be heard over distances of two or three miles, and even further under the right conditions, so that people in isolated areas could keep in contact with each other, transmit orders and so on and so save themselves those long and arduous journeys.

But a language that could be 'spoken'. We found that hard to believe and determined to put it to the test. Which we did one day in the Forest of Cedro.

We went there with a friend, Antonio Placencia, and met some woodmen who had agreed to give a demonstration. We had heard whistling on several occasions on the trip up to the forest, and our friend told us that the men whom we were to meet were being advised of our approach. And they were waiting for us when we arrived at the agreed rendezvous.

Introductions and preliminaries over, we set about the task of satisfying our curiosity. We had the men placed in positions where they were some distance apart and completely hidden so that it was impossible for them to signal each other in any way. Then we put them through rigorous tests for something like two hours – and not simple little commands like 'Take off your hat', 'Light a cigarette', and so on; we had them carry out a series of orders, some quite intricate and involved. Then we made it harder by asking questions that required long, and sometimes complicated, answers. Antonio, also hidden so that he could not see them, or be seen by them transmitted our questions in Spanish.

And in all that testing we had but one failure; a question beyond their understanding, and which they could not have answered even if it had been given in plain language. And in listening to the simplest questions and answers, we could on occasions, distinguish the rhythm of the actual words in their whistling.

The *silbadores* – as the practitioners of the *silbo* are called – use a variety of methods in their 'talking'. Some simply whistle with the tongue between the teeth; others use their fingers, some the first and second fingers of one hand, others a finger and thumb and so on. Some try to extend their range by cupping a hand around the mouth. But all are equally effective. We were told that children generally learned the *silbo* from their parents and so were, in a way 'bilingual'.

Unfortunately, the *silbo* is now fast dying out. In fact, it has long since virtually disappeared from the urban areas, and even in country districts is now little practiced except among the older people. What with telephones, radio, television, better communications and so forth, what real need is there for it? None, perhaps. But surely it is worth preserving as an ancient craft or art. Arts and crafts such as pottery, weaving, carving and so on are carefully preserved in most countries, so why not such an unusual one as this? People to whom we mentioned this seemed interested – but not particularly enthusiastic.

We did say to one official that it would prove a good tourist attraction, especially if steps were taken to ensure that visitors could have no reason to think they were being 'taken in'. The suggestion received a rather lukewarm reception; after all, it was such an old fashioned thing of little interest to modern tourists, he protested.

A pity. It would provide such an attraction – and would preserve an ancient custom. Let us hope that someone gives the idea some serious thought before it is too late and there are no *silbadores* left.

11. El Hierro

El Hierro, the 'Island of Iron', is the smallest (it has an area of 109 square miles) and most westerly of the Canaries. In fact, it is the most westerly land of the Old World, with nothing but ocean between it and the West Indies. So, in pre-Columbus days, this was the legendary land that really was the edge of the world. Its most south-westerly point was the last land that Columbus and his men saw before setting off into the unknown. Those seamen were unhappy at the thought of what lay before them, and the great discoverer had, by all accounts, some difficulty in persuading them to go on; and who knows what doubts he himself entertained as the last point of Hierro finally disappeared from sight.

Its geographic position led to its playing a prominent part in the setting of the zero degree of longitude in early days. Some Arab cartographers set that meridian on Hierro long before it was even known to the western world – which does seem somewhat unusual. Later the island was officially designated as the western extremity of the Old World – all beyond was the New. And in 1634 a conference convened in Paris by Cardinal Richelieu set the meridian that passed through Hierro as zero – and this was made official by Louis XIII of France. But a little later it was described as being 20 degrees west of Paris, the French evidently establishing their capital as the pivotal meridian. For long it was the custom of various countries to set their own capitals as the zero of longitude.

It was not until an international conference held in

Washington in 1884 that the Greenwich meridian was declared the zero degree of longitude; a decision that was accepted by most countries although a number did not recognise the decision for some years.

Its isolation, however, did not prevent Hierro from being one of the first of the islands to be overrun by the Spanish. When Bethencourt landed there in 1403 the frightened natives made off into the interior, but were enticed back to the shore where they were seized and carried off into slavery; very few seem to have escaped. The island was held as a feudal possession of the Lords of Gomera until they finally conceded their rights completely to the Spanish crown in the late eighteenth century. Hierro virtually has no subsequent history, suffering few slave raids and no naval attacks as did the other islands of the group.

Its geographic position, and the absence of good anchorages, resulted also in its being, like Gomera, largely out of touch with the rest of the archipelago and the world, so that few foreigners visited it. This, combined with the fact that most of the aborigines were carried off in the early days, the language of the original Spanish settlers has remained more or less uncorrupted, so, according to the experts, Herrenos speak the purest Spanish of the islands. And although it now does have a good port, as well as an airport, the Herreños have not, as yet, shown their awareness of the outside world or to the prospects of tourism that is stirring the Gomeros today. For how long, one wonders.

Hierro is well named, for it does have an iron appearance. For the most part its cliffs rise steeply from the sea, and on approaching it by ship it looks rather grim and forbidding – how much more so must it have been to those mariners of old. There is little in the way of coastal flats or of beaches. The interior is largely a tableland where its capital, Valverde, is situated (Hierro is the only island of the group which still has its capital away from the coast) as are most of its dozen or so villages and hamlets, and where most of its inhabitants live, farming their small parcels of land. There are no rivers and little rainfall. the rain is carefully caught in tanks and small catchment areas and this, together with the heavy mists and dew, provides the moisture required for agriculture. The main crops are figs and some cereals, and there is a little cattle and goat raising, the pastures being quite good. There are also some fine pine forests, pleasant havens of shade and green.

Puerto de la Estaca, usually referred to simply as Estaca, the port of Valverde – and the only port on the island – is a hamlet of a couple of dozen or so houses perched on a hillside overlooking the tiny harbour. The harbour is protected on one side by a cliff face and a convenient rock fall, and on the other by the quay. Today the inter-island steamers berth at the quayside, which was not possible on our first visit. Then ships anchored in the middle of the harbour, 100 yards or so from the quay and passengers were ferried to the wharf in a small boat, usually loaded to the gunwhales. That trip safely accomplished (as, miraculously, it always was) we climbed into the rickety old bus for the six-mile journey up to Valverde. You had to be lucky to make it by taxi, as there was only one then, old and wheezy. Today things are a little better; passengers are disembarked on to the quay and there is a better bus and a few newer taxis.

Of course you can now go to Hierro by air; very much quicker, but, somehow, to us that method lacks the spice of adventure which we associate with a visit to this veritable outpost of civilisation.

But Valverde does not seem to have changed very much. True, it has grown somewhat, and has about one-third of the island's population of around 10,000 inhabitants, and has three pensions against the one it had on our first visit.

These offer reasonable accommodation at moderate prices – adequate for a short stay, and few visitors would want more than that. Hierro is not the place for ordinary holiday makers and travellers on a time budget, but well worth a short visit for those who are making a prolonged stay in the islands and have the time to spare. We must say we have enjoyed all our visits here – perhaps because we kept them fairly brief.

There is little or nothing for the visitor to see in Valverde, but it is the best – one might say only – base from which to tour the island. This can be done fairly comfortably in one day by taxi, although two are better; more if you want to get the 'feel' of the place. You can also do it by bus if you wish, although the services are somewhat limited; it is a small island with only about 100 miles of good road. But taxi is certainly the best bet. Actually there is nothing outstanding about Hierro and popular tourism is virtually non-existent – but another of the results of its isolation is that it provides attractions for those travellers who like to go off the beaten track and find the unusual.

About two miles from Valverde is a laurel tree which stands on the spot where another laurel, called El Garoe, existed in Guanche days, and was said to have magical qualities. Around this tree is woven one of the island's favourite legends.

This tells how sufficient water dripped from the leaves of El Garoe to provide many families (how many differs in various versions of the legend) with all the water they needed – a great boon in this dry climate. When the Spanish arrived they were perplexed as to the source of this water, but the natives, fearing for their supplies, covered the tree up and all were enjoined to secrecy. The Spanish, desperately short of water, were anxious to discover the location of the mysterious reservoir.

Then, as with so many such legends, the love story comes in. A young Guanche girl, naturally a princess or a chief's daughter, fell in love with a young Spaniard and he tried to persuade her to tell him where the precious water came from. She resisted his pleas but finally gave in and told him the secret – and the invaders took over the magic tree. Later the girl, remorseful, confessed to what she had done, was tried by the elders of the tribe and was convicted and executed.

The tree is said to have stood for another 200 years before being destroyed in a storm three centuries ago. There are drawings, said to have been made at the time, showing the natives catching the water in pottery vessels. Other stories tell of tanks under the tree that were still there only a few years ago and of which there are still traces. And a farmer claimed as late as 1948 that he had a laurel tree which yielded him a barrel of water a day. We have seen the drawings but never saw the remains of those ancient tanks; nor did we find the farmer who caught a barrel of water a day from his own laurel trees. Though, of course, we did meet people who knew him, but never could say where he was at that moment!

Some experts have said that owing to the heavy mists that frequently envelop the higher parts of Hierro it would be possible for it to condense on the laurel leaves and drip off on to the ground. A number of trees clustered together could, in such circumstances, cause a sufficient accumulation of water to produce good pastures.

Another strange aspect of Hierro is definitely not legend – although in the telling it may well appear to be so. One of the principal items of diet here are fresh figs, and Herreños will make a complete minor meal of this fruit combined with *gofio*. They are really marvellous figs, among the most delicious we have ever tasted. The fig trees, as in Lanzarote, are trained to grow outwards rather than upwards, principally to make the most of the precious moisture, and some may stretch out 30 or 40 feet or more in all directions.

Now fig trees are the most prized possessions of many Herreño families, and when a farmer dies an extensive tree might pass to several new owners. This may mean dividing the tree between several beneficiaries, each taking a certain number of branches. And so small are some of the allotments that a tree may spread to two or more properties, therefore be inherited by still more beneficiaries. But to complicate matters still further, it is argued that the land beneath a tree belongs to the owner of the tree. And when a tree has two, three or more owners, you have a postion which inevitably leads to a great deal of discord.

We will leave the Herreños to it – but no matter what discord those trees may cause, there is no doubt as to the quality of the figs.

The road to the west from Valverde leads through San Andres and La Frontera, two of the most important villages after Valverde, and Tigaday, where there is a curious church with a separate belfry. Not that this is unique in itself for we have seen a number in Britain, Europe and other parts of the world. But here the two are separated by some two hundred yards, the church at the bottom of a hill, the belfry at the top. We sought the reason and the priest gave us the answer.

When the church was built it was found that the belfry could not be seen from afar. In fact, it could not be seen until one had almost reached the church. Something that could not be tolerated. So the belfry was demolished and rebuilt at the top of the hill, more than 100 feet above the church. That made it visible from a considerable distance, some time before the church came into view. And so everybody was happy.

Further on is Sabinosa, the most westerly village of the Canaries. Here are thermal springs where the waters are said to beneficial and a rather small health resort has been established. It is not for foreigners, but rather locals looking for cures.

Beyond Sabinosa is the Ermita de los Reyes where the statue of the Virgin de los Reyes, the patron saint of the island, is kept; it is carried to Valverde during the annual festival held each May. From here it is less than a mile to a spot from which the Punta Orchilla, the most westerly point, that 'edge of the world', can be viewed, and from where a lighthouse beams it s light out into the limitless ocean.

Those interested in ancient and prehistoric rock carvings and inscriptions will find some of the best in the Canaries in caves in Hierro. All that they prove, say some experts, are that the islands were inhabited a long time ago, but not by whom. Their origins are mysterious and they have not yet been satisfactorily deciphered. There are some not far from Valverde, but the best are at Los Letteros, near the south coast. Most of the inscriptions are to be found in places difficult to reach, and those wishing to see them should enquire at the Cabildo as to where they are and the best way to get to them. Once away from the capital it is unlikely that you will find anyone who has any knowledge of English – or any other foreign language for that matter.

On the final night of our last visit to Hierro we made a comfortable journey from Valverde 2,000 feet down the hill to

catch our boat in good time. How different to the ride on our
first trip. After dinner there had been some singing and a little
folk dancing at the pension, and as the night wore on and
11.30 and sailing time approached no one seemed to be in the
least worried about the boat. Then, faintly, we heard its first
whistle indicating that departure time would be in about 20
minutes. Still no one seemed concerned, and five minutes
later, when we showed some signs of agitation, were told,
airily, 'Don't worry, there's plenty of time. It's only five
minutes to the port.'

Five minutes to do six miles down that rough and rutted
road, cliffs on one side and a long drop into the sea on the
other. We shuddered at the prospect.

Then there were two blasts from the steamer's whistle, and
suddenly all was activity and the six passengers who were
sailing – six others as well as ourselves, that is – hurried out
and we all piled into that rickety old taxi – a terrible squash.
With a screech we were off and then followed one of the most
hair-raising rides we have ever made. The old taxi coughed
and spluttered, bounced and swerved, groaned and rattled as
we careered down with ever-increasing speed. Somehow we
stayed on the road – but we will never know how. And as the
last warning whistle was sounded we came to a violent halt
where the tender waited for us, the attendant bidding us to
hurry.

We scrambled on board and the steamer was off with a final
'hoot' as the last of us tumbled onto the deck.

We gathered that such a last minute drive down from
Valverde was the usual procedure every steamer night.

It was very dark and few lights twinkled on the quay – and
none from the houses of Estaca – as we steamed away after our
first visit to 'the edge of the world'.

Glossary

Some Spanish words in common usage in the islands which it may be helpful to know.

autopista	main highway
avenida	avenue
barranco	ravine or old river bed
balneario	swimming pool
caldera	crater
calle	street
capilla	chapel
carretera	highway
casa	house
ciudad	city
cumbre	summit of mountain
entrada	entrance
ermita	chapel or hermitage
finca	farm or farmhouse
fonda	inn
iglesia	church
malpais	bad lands, country covered with lava
mirador	look out, viewing point
muelle	mole or quay
nieve	snow
patio	courtyard
pico	peak (of mountain)
pinar	pine forest
platano	banana
playa	beach
plaza	a square
pueblo	village or town
rambla	boulevard
salida	exit
sierra	range of mountains
valle	valley
villa	town

Acknowledgements

We would like to thank the tourist authorities on all the islands for their assistance over the years, especially Señor José Santana of Santa Cruz de Tenerife, and Señor José Luis Gonzalez of Las Palmas de Grand Canary. Also Señor Antonio Sahagún Pool of the Spanish National Tourist Office in London.

Our thanks go to Mr Sydney Smith, of the Union Castle Line, for his help on many occasions during the past years; and to Mr Wilfred Jones, chairman of Cosmos Tours, for his co-operation and assistance on both major islands.

And to all our friends in the Canary Islands, whom we hope to see again in the future.

INDEX